Improving Project Performance Using the PRINCE2™ Maturity Model (P2MM)

London: TSO

Published by TSO (The Stationery Office) and available from:

Online
www.tsoshop.co.uk

Mail, Telephone, Fax & E-mail
TSO
PO Box 29, Norwich NR3 1GN
Telephone orders/General enquiries: 0870 600 5522
Fax orders: 0870 600 5533
E-mail: customer.services@tso.co.uk
Textphone: 0870 240 3701

TSO Shops
16 Arthur Street, Belfast BT1 4GD
028 9023 8451 Fax 028 9023 5401
71 Lothian Road, Edinburgh EH3 9AZ
0870 606 5566 Fax 0870 606 5588

TSO@Blackwell and other Accredited Agents

A CIP catalogue record for this book is available from the British Library

A Library of Congress CIP catalogue record has been applied for

First published 2007

ISBN 9780113310319

Printed in the United Kingdom by The Stationery Office, London.

N5523802 c20 7/07

Contents

Foreword

The 1990s saw a dramatic increase in the number of people with the job title 'Project Manager' as organisations addressed the problem of an ever-changing world through 'Managing by Projects'. Many organisations adopted the PRINCE2™ method as a means to gain some consistency of project management approach across their now swelling ranks of Project Managers.

With both an increasing need for Project Managers and an increasing number of people claiming to be Project Managers, many organisations based their recruitment and development strategies on certification of project management competence. Having a PRINCE2 Practitioner certificate became an indication of competence (even though it is only an indicator of knowledge). Gaining a PRINCE2 Practitioner certificate does not automatically make someone a great Project Manager. There are numerous soft skills that good Project Managers require (such as communication, decision-making, problem-solving, leadership, facilitation, negotiation, etc.).

Experience has shown that successful implementation of a project management method requires more than just training your Project Managers and producing a few templates. A successful organisation requires processes, technology, policies and standards for project management – which also need to be integrated with other management systems for them to work effectively and efficiently.

In the absence of an organisation-wide project infrastructure, project results depend entirely on the availability of certain high-performing individuals. This does not necessarily provide the basis for long-term or consistent project performance.

However, such infrastructure doesn't establish itself overnight. It typically requires a programme of change to institutionalise good project management practice. Therefore it is not surprising that the more advanced organisations are now asking themselves, 'Where have we got to and what more do we need to do?'

This is where the PRINCE2 Maturity Model (P2MM)[1] can help. It describes the project-related activities within Key Process Areas (KPAs) that contribute to achieving successful outcomes. P2MM recognises not only the project management activities being carried out at the individual project level, but also those activities within an organisation that build and maintain an infrastructure of effective project approaches and management practices.

By undertaking a maturity assessment against an industry standard model, such as P2MM, an organisation will be able to verify what it has achieved, where its strengths and weaknesses are, and then identify a prioritised action plan to take the organisation to an improved level of capability. Organisations can also use P2MM as a benchmark to compare their maturity against others or against themselves at an earlier point in time.

> We are all aware of the vital role that good project management plays in the effective and efficient delivery of goods and services. While PRINCE2 gives us a proven, world-leading methodology, it does not tell organisations how good they are at project management. The PRINCE2 Maturity Model fills this gap, providing a way of testing how well the method is applied and where improvement may be beneficial. It is a significant step forward in building project management skills and ensuring greater success in delivering products and services.
> (Neil Glover,
> Procurement Policy, Office of Government Commerce)

The TSO maturity mark on the back cover will help you decide if this publication is positioned at the appropriate level for your requirements and provide a route map to progress with embedding OGC guidance.

Improving Project Performance using P2MM is level 3 and 4. Level 3 is Defined (institutionalised) – OGC guidance is defined/confirmed as a standard business process. Level 4 is Managed (quantified) – process management and measurement takes place.

For more information on the TSO maturity mark and how it can help you, please visit www.best-management-practice.com

Acknowledgements

TSO and the authors would like to thank the following people for their help in putting together this publication.

Contributors

Bernard Abbott	Outperform UK Ltd
Fiona Bradshaw	Financial Services Authority
Heather Butler	Financial Services Authority
Max Carter	London Borough of Waltham Forest
Tony Church	Sun Microsystems Inc.
Kevin Fletcher	Manchester City Council
Jo Lane	Stockport Metropolitan Borough Council
Graham Ovenden	EDF Energy
Sue Vowler	Project Angels
Dolores Wolfe	EDF Energy

Reviewers

Andrew Ball	Audit Commission
Sean Barrett	Department for Constitutional Affairs
Mike Bennett	Independent
Brian Coombes	The Projects Group
John Herd	Advantek AG
Stephanie Howe	Pension Service IS IT Directorate
Tony Levene	Quality Projects (Consulting) Ltd
Bruce McNaughton	Customer Driven Solutions
Simon Marling	UK Debt Management Office
Angela Murphy	Camden Council
Tim Reeks	HM Revenue & Customs
Martin Rother	QRP M.M.I. GmbH
David Warley	Outperform UK Ltd

Introduction

1

1 Introduction

1.1 PURPOSE

The purpose of this guide is to help organisations gain full value from the PRINCE2 method by providing practical advice on using the OGC's PRINCE2 Maturity Model (P2MM)[1]. The guide will show how P2MM can be used:

- To help implement PRINCE2 (first-time users)
- To re-invigorate existing PRINCE2 implementations
- To help organisations improve their project performance by going beyond training and templates (i.e. overcoming the issue of PRINCE In Name Only – PINO*)
- As a benchmark to assess organisational capability, plan improvements and to measure the success of such improvement initiatives
- As a means for external recognition of organisational (rather than individual) PRINCE2 capability via the APM Group Ltd's accreditation assessments
- As part of a wider goal to improve Portfolio, Programme and Project Management performance using the OGC's P3M3[2] (see Chapter 7).

The guide is intended for those people responsible for or involved in the implementation/adoption of PRINCE2:

- Head of Projects (or equivalent)
- Project/Programme Office Manager (or equivalent)
- Project Manager (of a PRINCE2 implementation project)
- Quality Manager
- Internal Auditor
- Consultant (internal and external).

1.2 HOW TO USE THIS GUIDE

This book is a companion to the PRINCE2 manual[3], and assumes that readers are already familiar with the PRINCE2 method. No prior knowledge of maturity models is required. However, those people unfamiliar with maturity models should read section 1.4 and Appendix B.

> The PRINCE2™ Maturity Model (P2MM) is available from the OGC website. Extracts from the model included in this manual are denoted like this and also appear in tinted boxes. Extracts/quotes from other sources also appear like this.

Chapter 2 provides an overview of how to plan performance improvements using P2MM.

Chapters 3, 4 and 5 provide an explanation of the Key Process Areas (KPAs) within the three levels of the maturity model. Each KPA is organised under the headings: Purpose, Key Practices, What does this KPA mean?, Why is this KPA important?, How can this KPA be implemented? and Examples.

Chapter 6 describes P2MM assessment methods and accreditation.

Chapter 7 introduces the Portfolio, Programme and Project Management Maturity Model (P3M3).

Appendix A contains checklists that can be used to self-assess maturity.

Appendix B provides further information on maturity models and P2MM.

Appendix C provides some background information on the authors of this book.

---

* It is unclear from where the term PINO originates, but its characteristics and dangers were presented to the Best Practice User Group conference by Andrew Ball from the Audit Commission in 2005.

1.3 PRINCE2 10 YEARS ON

Before looking at the PRINCE2 Maturity Model, let's remind ourselves of what PRINCE2 encompasses.

PRINCE2 was launched by the UK Government in 1996 and has since become the most widely used project management method worldwide. At the end of 2006 there were more than 250,000 certified Project Managers who had sat and passed the PRINCE2 Practitioner exam. PRINCE2 Practitioners can now be found in all seven continents (even in Antarctica where PRINCE2 has been used by the British Antarctic Survey since 2001). The PRINCE2 manual is also available in several languages.

PRINCE2 is now more than a just manual. When people say 'We are using PRINCE2', they don't mean that they are using the manual. They mean that they direct, manage or participate on a project that follows (some of) the processes, components and techniques embodied in the PRINCE2 manual.

PRINCE2 has become a way of delivering projects. It has become the international language for project management. It has become a community, and a global community at that. The community comprises:

- The UK Government (PRINCE2 is owned by the Office of Government Commerce – OGC)
- A documented method (the manual, now in its 4th edition)[3]
- An accreditation body (the APM Group Ltd)
- The official publisher for the OGC (TSO) with nearly 30 publications relating to PRINCE2
- 120+ accredited training organisations, providing training around the globe in 17 languages
- 15+ Accredited Consulting Organisations
- Software tools (there were 52 tools supporting PRINCE2 listed in *Project Manager Today*'s December 2006 PM Software Tool sourcebook)

- An official user group (the Best Practice User Group – BPUG) and numerous other user groups covering more than 10 countries
- Numerous on-line discussion forums dedicated to PRINCE2 (e.g. ecademy, APMG-ICP, Yahoo!)
- More than 250,000 certified practitioners worldwide.

The number of people using PRINCE2 is many times the number of people certified to Practitioner Level and its reach is evident in that a Google™ search will show that there are more than 1.6 million pages on the worldwide web that reference PRINCE2 – much more than any other method.

While the PRINCE2 manual is owned and maintained by the UK Government, several other governments are now recommending its use (for example, the Netherlands, Denmark, Germany) and it has been adopted by the United Nations Development Programme as part of their global framework for managing projects. Its use extends beyond governments and institutions as it has been adopted by the private sector with some vigour. PRINCE2 has also moved beyond its IT origin and is used for R&D projects, construction projects, product development projects, marketing projects, business transformation projects and many more.

While this is all very laudable, the PRINCE2 phenomenon is dampened by the fact that for every well-run project using PRINCE2, there are a number of poorly run projects using PINO (PRINCE In Name Only). Common issues observed with PINO projects are:

- The start-up phase is rushed or missed and the organisation jumps straight to producing a Project Initiation Document (PID). Poor or incomplete planning results in poor projects.
- Project Boards are not effective – escalations may go into a black hole, the Project Board refuses to baseline the scope, etc.

- Gantt charts form the basis of project planning instead of Product Breakdown Structures. Without Product Descriptions, PRINCE2's quality management processes and techniques do not work.
- Tolerances are not set or are limited to time and cost only – it is unclear what delegated authority people have or under what conditions they should escalate to the next level. Project Issues or overruns can come as a surprise.
- Projects are all single stage (or 'phases' are used to avoid doing an End Stage Review). This reduces control, making planning difficult.
- PIDs are simply a 'cut and paste' from the last project – they are not read or followed and only serve as shelf-ware.
- There is a low level of 'business' involvement because it is regarded as a 'technical' method – the project outputs might not deliver the desired outcomes.

The 'hit and miss' nature of how well PRINCE2 is applied is one of the reasons why the OGC produced the PRINCE2 Maturity Model (P2MM). P2MM describes the infrastructure an organisation should have in order to gain full value from adopting and using PRINCE2 as a corporate standard. P2MM also provides a roadmap for implementation, which can help organisations accelerate their path to PRINCE2 maturity.

1.4 WHAT ARE MATURITY MODELS?

A maturity model is a structured collection of elements that describe characteristics of effective processes. A maturity model provides:

- A place to start
- The benefit of a community's prior experiences
- A common language and a shared vision
- A framework for prioritizing actions
- A way to define what improvement means for your organization.

A maturity model can be used as a benchmark for assessing different organizations for equivalent comparison.

Source – Wikipedia, February 2007

Maturity models are management tools designed to help organisations implement effective processes in a given management discipline (e.g. project management). Maturity models are developed on the basis that organisations do not move from zero capability to optimum capability instantaneously. Instead, organisations progress along a journey of maturity.

Maturity models generally describe five levels of maturity:

1 Initial (chaotic, ad hoc, heroic) – the starting point for use of a new process
2 Repeatable (process discipline) – the process is used repeatedly
3 Defined (institutionalised) – the process is defined/confirmed as a standard business process
4 Managed (quantified) – process management and measurement take place
5 Optimising (process improvement) – deliberate process optimisation/improvement.

Each level contains a number of Key Process Areas (KPAs). A KPA is a cluster of best practices, which when implemented collectively satisfy a set of goals considered important for making significant improvement in that area (for example, risk management is a KPA in P2MM). The lower level KPAs need to be in place for the higher level KPAs to be effective. This hierarchical structure is the essence of the value of maturity models – analysing strengths and weaknesses by KPA enables organisations to break down a broad process improvement goal into manageable and prioritised tasks. In this way they can address the lowest level 'weak' KPAs first.

Maturity models can be used to assess where you are on the maturity journey (therefore what to do next) or can be used as a roadmap to help organisations implement a capability from new.

1.5 THE PRINCE2 MATURITY MODEL

The purpose of P2MM is to enable organisations to gauge, by assessment, their maturity in the use of the PRINCE2™ project management method.

The model can be used:

■ To understand the key practices that are part of an effective organisational process to manage projects
■ To identify the key practices that need to be embedded within the organisation to achieve the next level of maturity.

Source – P2MM[1]

The PRINCE2 Maturity Model describes a set of KPAs required for the effective implementation and use of PRINCE2 within an organisation. This is P2MM's core value: while the PRINCE2 manual describes how to manage a single project, it does not include any processes on how to embed PRINCE2. By contrast, P2MM does.

P2MM describes Key Practices aligned to the PRINCE2 processes and components to enable repeatable application of the method (Level 2 KPAs) and goes further to describe the Key Practices required to institutionalise the method (Level 3 KPAs) as a standard business process for managing projects. These include assigning ownership (KPA 3.1), tailoring the method (KPA 3.2), training (KPA 3.3), integrating with other management systems (KPA 3.4) and quality assurance mechanisms (KPA 3.5) to gain a continuous improvement process.

Figure 1.1 illustrates the KPAs within P2MM. Level 2 KPAs concern the application of PRINCE2 at the project level. Level 3 KPAs concern the processes and infrastructure required at the organisation level to ensure that application of PRINCE2 is specific to the organisation, consistently applied and continuously improved based on actual feedback.

PRINCE2 addresses only a part of the wider project management body of knowledge. In a similar way P2MM provides the 'method' element of the wider Project Management Maturity Model (P1M3) with KPAs at Levels 1, 2 and 3 only.

P2MM can be used as a stand-alone model or it can be used in conjunction with the OGC's Portfolio, Programme and Project Management Maturity Model: P1M3 (projects), P2M3 (+programmes) and P3M3 (+portfolios). See section 6.3.4 and Chapter 7 for details on P1M3, P2M3 and P3M3. This enables organisations to assess their maturity in PRINCE2, in project management generically or in both.

Figure 1.2 illustrates how P2MM is a subset of P1M3, with KPAs at Levels 2 and 3 only. P2MM references P1M3 for the Level 1 KPAs, since the Key Practices described at Level 1 are not addressed by the PRINCE2 method.

Organisations can use the checklists at the end of this book to self-assess their level of maturity or they can choose to undergo an external assessment using Registered Consultants. Registered Consultants are able to conduct an accreditation assessment that can result in a certificate from the OGC's accreditation partner the APM Group Ltd (the APM Group), verifying an organisation's level of maturity (see section 6.3). The benefits of external assessment are:

■ A known and independently verified maturity level
■ Value-added advice from experienced Registered Consultants
■ An ability to compare your organisation with others
■ A certificate showing your organisation's competence (for general marketing purposes and for responding to tenders).

Figure 1.1 P2MM Key Process Areas

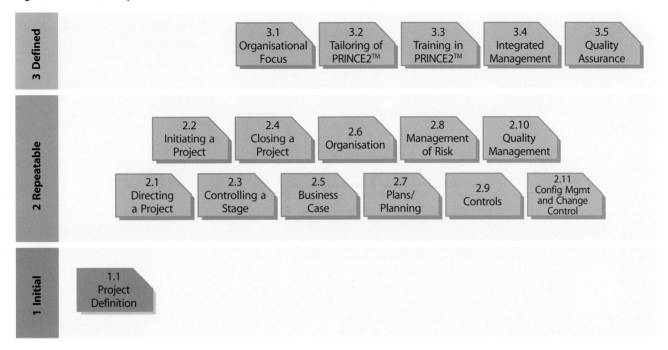

1.6 BENEFITS OF USING P2MM

An assessment [against P2MM] can be undertaken for organisations that deliver projects internally or those that provide a project management service.

The main benefit for organisations that deliver internal projects is that they will be able to identify their strengths and areas for improvement and build an action plan to improve their effectiveness in the use of PRINCE2™. This will lead to PRINCE2™ being embedded within the organisation and delivery of the full benefits of using a structured project management method.

For those organisations that provide a project management service, in addition to the above benefits they will also be able to provide evidence to their clients and prospective clients of their level of maturity in the use of PRINCE2™. This could provide a marketing advantage.

Source – P2MM[1]

Figure 1.2 P2MM maturity levels compared with P1M3 levels

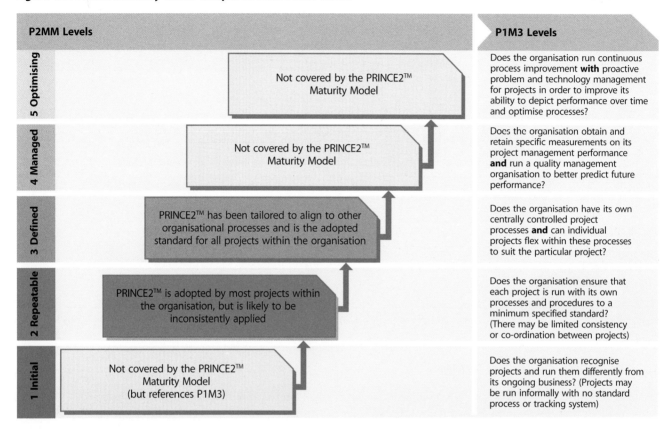

P2MM has the following uses:

- Provides a benchmark of current capability
- Enables complex 'change' to be broken down into more manageable and achievable tasks
- Optimises investment in capability by identifying those KPAs that, if improved, will yield greatest improvement in performance through:
  - An understanding of your strengths and weaknesses in project management
  - A prioritised roadmap of what's needed in order to improve
- Provides a method for continuous improvement

- Assists benefits realisation for investment in project management capability (e.g. before and after measures)
- Can be used as a readiness assessment before implementing tools (i.e. the tools should support your target KPAs only)
- Can be used to compare autonomous business units or departments within your organisation and to share best practices from each
- Can help with re-organisations (e.g. after a merger or acquisition) to decide which set of handbooks/processes to adopt as the corporate method

- Can be used by buyers to evaluate and compare suppliers' capability
- Can be used by suppliers to demonstrate organisational capability (rather than individual capability) as a differentiator
- Enables your organisation to meet four out of 11 principles of project governance as recommended by the Association for Project Management (APM)[4]. A further six principles can be met with additions. See section 2.2.3 for more details.

P2MM can be used to assess existing implementations of PRINCE2 in order to determine what else can be done to gain more value from it, or it can be used to help organisations implementing PRINCE2 formally for the first time. In both cases, the principal benefit is that it will maximise the impact of any investment you make in improving capability.

Improvement planning using P2MM

2

2 Improvement planning using P2MM

2.1 PERFORMANCE IMPROVEMENT PROCESS

The case for undertaking improvements based on data from a PRINCE2 maturity assessment will need to be clearly understood within your business context. It is all very well trying to reach the status of 'strong' in KPA 2.4 'Closing a Project', but what problem are you trying to fix? Gaining P2MM Level 3 maturity is a means to an end. The end result is 'better projects', so what does 'better projects' mean for your organisation? What's required to get there? Can the improvements be measured? How can you make sure those problems don't come back? Figure 2.1 shows a suggested approach to using P2MM to drive performance improvements.

The approach below is based on the premise that you need to understand current capability in order to determine how to improve it. By undertaking an assessment based on P2MM you will gain an understanding of your organisation's strengths and weaknesses, which will help you to prioritise those items that need addressing first. If there is a large gap between where you are today and where you'd like to be, set realistic goals and gain maturity in just a few KPAs before addressing others. It is important when planning improvements to understand how you will measure their impact. Therefore an important aspect of maturity models is measurement. Establishing an ongoing measurement capability means that a continuous improvement cycle can be achieved.

Figure 2.1 Suggested approach to improving performance using P2MM

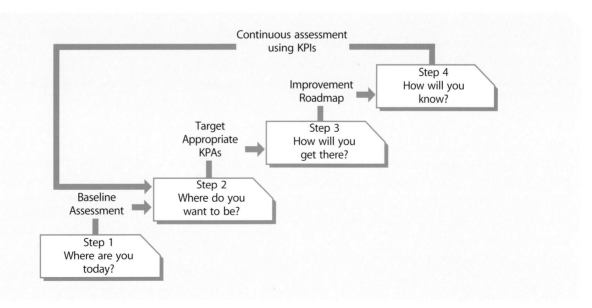

2.1.1 Step 1 – Where are you today?

In order to identify a prioritised roadmap for process improvement it is important to understand which KPAs you currently perform well in and which KPAs are causing performance issues. Maturity modelling applies the concept that there's little point in fixing things that are not broken or that are not causing problems.

Additionally, for large organisations it is likely that you have islands of good practice. Consider what it is that department X does differently from department Y or Z. It may be that you have many of the KPAs covered but not universally across the organisation. Adopting good practice from within your own organisation can significantly accelerate adoption rates and performance improvement.

The best way to understand current capability is to conduct a baseline assessment against the maturity model, through a process of inspection and structured interviews. The assessment could either be a self-assessment (see section 6.2.3) or a formal assessment using a Registered Consultant (see section 6.4).

Figure 2.2 shows the maturity result by each Key Process Area for a small technology company.

In this example, the organisation is struggling to close projects properly (2.4 and 2.9). End Project Reports are rarely done and post-project reviews are either not planned or do not take place. As a result, the organisation is not verifying whether the business benefits are being gained (2.5) and are not learning lessons (3.1 and 3.5). A systemic cause of this problem is that Project Boards (2.1) consistently negotiate down the project management resource allocated to projects in order to help spread an overworked pool of Project Managers (3.1 commitment).

When undertaking a maturity assessment, find out what metrics your organisation already collects. You may be able link process maturity with project performance, for example:

- Do you carry out customer satisfaction surveys to find out what customers think of you as a supplier? What results are you getting? Perhaps your customers think that you are not giving them timely information about a project's performance (e.g. 8 out of 10 customers are saying this).
- Do you have a list of projects that have failed in some way? Can you analyse this list to understand any common causes of these failures? (e.g. do all projects under-estimate the resources required?).
- How much is your organisation spending on creating project methods? If you have a number of disparate parts to your organisation, is there duplication of effort? How much can be saved by having one common approach?

2.1.2 Step 2 – Where do you want to be?

Decide what you would like to change. For each change, try to articulate the precise benefit in measurable terms and then choose just a few areas for improvement. When looking at the Business Case, choose areas of change that have the greatest business benefit for your organisation, and then set targets for the performance measures you would like to achieve. But remember, not all organisations need to be at the highest level of maturity. The ideal maturity level for an organisation will depend on how important programmes and projects are to the organisation's overall performance.

If you are an R&D organisation developing aerospace technology for governments for example, your organisation's performance is likely to be highly dependent on your programme and project management capability. If, by contrast, you are a retailer then your organisation's overall performance is likely to be less dependent on programme and project management capability.

The output from Step 1 will help to identify some realistic goals. For example, there are 11 KPAs that need to be addressed to get to Level 2 maturity. If the initial assessment has shown that six of the 11 are ok, then a realistic goal would be to develop the five weak KPAs into strong KPAs within six months to consolidate at Level 2 before addressing how to get to Level 3.

Figure 2.3 shows that the adopted strategy focused on ensuring a commitment to provide sufficient project management resources (3.1), that Business Cases are only approved if they included resources for the orderly close-down of a project (2.4) and that the closure activities are monitored as part of a gateway process (2.9 and 3.4). It was decided that Management of Risk (2.8), Quality Management (2.10), Integrated Management (3.4) and Quality Assurance (3.5) would have to wait until the priority areas were resolved.

2.1.3 Step 3 – How will you get there?

A recommended approach to improve process capability is to appoint process owners for the areas to be addressed. For example, you could appoint one person to drive the improvements in Business Case and Project Board-related processes, and another person to drive improvements in Project Controls. An improvement roadmap should be produced showing the priority of the KPAs to be addressed and the set of initiatives that will improve them. The improvement roadmap should be used to drive and measure progress.

It is important to recognise that if you are changing processes, policies, standards, job descriptions or reporting structures then you will be changing how some people work. Therefore, as with any initiative that affects people's current working practices, power or authority, it should be treated as a change initiative. If the change is likely to be significant, it is recommended that you establish a change programme to help with the transition. Methods such as Six Sigma and IDEAL provide useful techniques and are complementary to Managing Successful Programmes (MSP) as the management method.

If implementing PRINCE2 (formally) for the first time, the two most important KPAs to focus on are Project Definition (KPA 1.1) and Organisational Focus (KPA 3.1). The purpose of Organisational Focus is to establish the organisational responsibility for the adoption and ongoing use of PRINCE2 with the aim of improving the organisation's overall project management capability. If this ownership is lacking, implementation will be very difficult. A proactive approach to the Level 3 KPAs will help consolidate existing capabilities across the Level 2 KPAs.

2.1.4 Step 4 – How will you know?

To increase capability, organisations need to collect metrics in order to provide a platform for continuous improvement. Therefore, regardless of your baseline maturity, it is recommended that the improvement roadmap identifies which metrics should be collected to demonstrate performance improvement.

The establishment of Key Performance Indicators (KPIs) will not only enable organisations to determine when they have achieved their goal but can also be used to prove the Business Case for the process improvement journey, i.e. what is your return on the capability investment?

If your KPIs show that you have achieved your current maturity goal, then you may wish to consider gaining accreditation for that level of maturity (for recognition or for marketing purposes) or you may wish to repeat the exercise to determine what is required to get to the next level of maturity.

Finally, consider publishing your results – internally and externally. Demonstrating corporate pride in achieving improved performance can be an accelerator for further improvement.

Figure 2.2 Before – Baseline Assessment Result

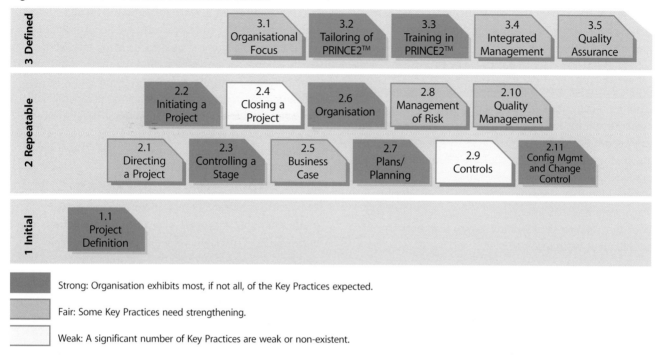

Strong: Organisation exhibits most, if not all, of the Key Practices expected.

Fair: Some Key Practices need strengthening.

Weak: A significant number of Key Practices are weak or non-existent.

Figure 2.3 After – Maturity Goal

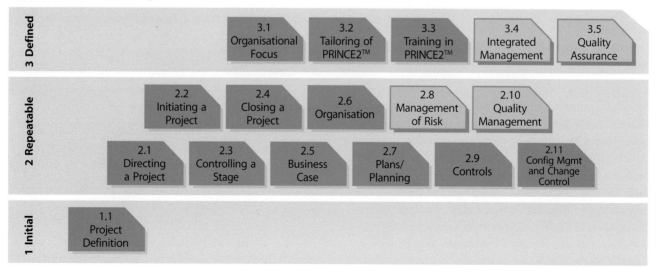

2.2 THE BUSINESS CASE

2.2.1 What's the proof?

The Software Engineering Institute (SEI) has collected metrics for organisations that have applied for accreditation against CMMI® (applications development). The metrics show a return on investment ranging from 2:1 to 27:1 with an average of just under 5:1. SEI's research shows that organisations that improve their process maturity gain:

- Improved schedule and budget predictability
- Increased productivity
- Improved quality (as measured by defects)
- Increased customer satisfaction
- Improved employee morale
- Increased return on investment
- Decreased cost of quality.

At present there are no comparable figures for improvements made resulting from the implementation of P2MM. The P2MM was in draft release until February 2006, and it is too early to have such performance data. The Accredited Consulting Organisations (ACOs) are working with the APM Group to collate this data.

The National Audit Office report, Delivering Successful IT-Enabled Business Change[5] (November 2006) covered an assessment of 20 successful public sector and private sector large-scale projects to identify their common characteristics. A recurring 'key success factor' identified in the report was, 'Building capacity and capability [in project and programme management]'.

2.2.2 Results so far

UK telecoms company: By the end of the project a £1.2 million saving was directly attributable to the increase in maturity, with projected benefits of a further £16 million per annum.

Global IT organisation: The Business Case projected highly conservative direct cost savings of $2 million per annum across the company. Target areas of focus were:

- Improved customer satisfaction
- Support for corporate financial compliance standards
- Common approach to managing engagements across the organisation
- Consistent look-and-feel to all documentation
- Provision of accurate information about the status of a project in a timely manner.

Company X: This organisation had an average product development lifecycle of 400 days when it started to introduce PRINCE2 using the maturity model approach. Additionally, its project management metrics showed that only 24% of projects met the time, cost and quality targets agreed during initiation. When PRINCE2 was fully embedded in the organisation the average product development lifecycle was reduced to less than 180 days and 80% of projects met the agreed time, cost and quality targets. This gave the organisation a significant competitive advantage over its peers within the industry. The structured implementation of PRINCE2 also increased the quality of data on the organisation's Project Register. This enabled the Projects Review Group to optimise its portfolio with confidence, knowing that they were making decisions based on reliable data. The compound effect of all these improvements also increased the morale of the project management group as the wider organisation gained a better understanding of projects and the value of a good Project Manager.

2.2.3 Improved governance

By achieving P2MM Level 3 your organisation will be able to meet four out of 11 principles of project management governance as recommended by the Association for Project Management (APM)[4]. A further six principles can be met with some minor additions to your PRINCE2 implementation.

2.2.4 Developing your own Business Case

In the introduction to this chapter we established that gaining P2MM Level 3 maturity is only a means to an end: The end result is 'better projects'. Understanding what 'better projects' means for your organisation in financial terms will help you build your business case.

For example do you know:

- How many projects are 'live' in your organisation?
- How many Project Managers you have?
- How many qualified Project Managers you have?
- How many people work on projects? For how much of their working week?
- What percent of projects overrun, and by how much on average?
- What percent of projects overspend, and by how much on average (money or days' effort)?
- The amount of re-work on projects, as a percentage of the baseline budget (money or days' effort)?
- The correlation between project management performance and customer satisfaction?
- The average time it takes to launch a new product?
- The amount of time Project Managers spend collating information to cut and paste into a Highlight Report?
- The amount of time Project Board members spend cutting information from Highlight Reports and pasting it into Business Unit reports?
- And so on…

The answers to these questions will help you quantify the potential financial gains that better projects will provide for your organisation. An initial understanding of these metrics is required in order to measure the improvements.

You should be looking for a positive return on investment (ROI). A simple ROI calculation:

ROI % = 100* (cost savings + performance improvements – incremental costs)/Incremental costs

Where:

- Cost savings = less re-work, less duplication, less management intervention, etc.
- Performance improvements = more projects for the same money, better outcomes, etc.
- Incremental costs = cost of implementation + cost of support.

This is a simple calculation and would need to be applied over a specified period for it to make sense (one year, two years?). The main point here is that whatever you decide are the cost savings, performance improvements and incremental costs, they need to be measured and should be used to define the scope and priority of the improvement project.

Table 2.1 APM's governance of project management principles

Number	Governance of project management principles	P2MM Level 3
1	The board has overall responsibility for governance of project management.	Partial
2	The roles, responsibilities and performance criteria for the governance of project management are clearly defined.	✓
3	Disciplined governance arrangements, supported by appropriate methods and controls, are applied throughout the project life cycle.	Partial
4	A coherent and supportive relationship is demonstrated between the overall business strategy and the project portfolio.	NA
5	All projects have an approved plan containing authorisation points at which the Business Case is reviewed and approved. Decisions made at authorisation points are recorded and communicated.	✓
6	Members of delegated authorisation bodies have sufficient representation, competence, authority and resources to enable them to make appropriate decisions.	Partial
7	The project Business Case is supported by relevant and realistic information that provides a reliable basis for making authorisation decisions.	✓
8	The board or its delegated agents decide when independent scrutiny of projects and project management systems is required, and implement such scrutiny accordingly.	Partial
9	There are clearly defined criteria for reporting project status and for the escalation of risks and issues to the levels required by the organisation.	✓
10	The organisation fosters a culture of improvement and of frank internal disclosure of project information.	Partial
11	Project stakeholders are engaged at a level that is commensurate with their importance to the organisation and in a manner that fosters trust.	Partial

Source – *Directing Change: A Guide to Governance of Project Management* (reprinted with minor revisions 2005), APM Governance SIG. © Association for Project Management, 2004. Reproduced with permission.

Level 1 maturity

3

3   Level 1 maturity

Figure 3.1 Level 1 organisation

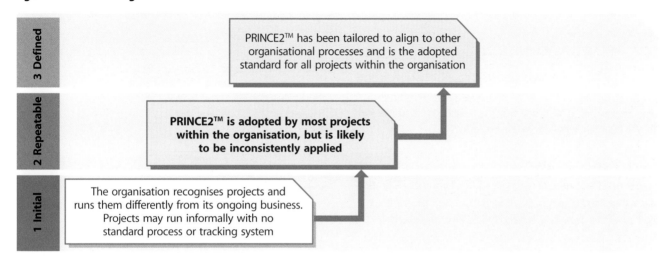

3.1   THE LEVEL 1 ORGANISATION

This level is sometimes referred to as the heroic level because projects are often delivered through the personal heroics and efforts of Project Managers and their teams. They tend to be delivered in spite of the organisation rather than because of it.

In the Level 1 organisation, project management tends to be ad hoc in its application. Some projects might use PRINCE2 because the Project Manager happens to be a PRINCE2 Practitioner or used it with a previous employer. Other Project Managers may be completely untrained – the Accidental Project Manager – appointed because they know the most about the project content. The Accidental Project Manager is likely to be a subject expert (e.g. IT Designer, Purchasing Manager, teaching professional), but may not have relevant skills or experience to plan, lead and control a project.

The measure of success at this level tends to be when the desired outputs are delivered on time, to specification and within budget. This may happen from time to time, but it does not happen consistently. On occasion it is unclear whether these targets are met, as no timescales, specifications or budgets were defined at the start.

Level 1 organisations are typically those that are exposed to projects for the first time. There is a realisation that project management is different from line management and needs to be treated in a different way to business-as-usual operations. This realisation often comes when organisations first start to appoint people to lead projects and give them the title of Project Manager. Unfortunately, Level 1 organisations are unlikely to have functioning Project Boards.

To progress to Level 2, an organisation should recognise the projects it is undertaking, have agreed objectives for what's expected of the project and appoint an owner to authorise the necessary budget and resources required to meet the objectives. The Project Manager needs sufficient skill to be able to define the outputs and plan the activities (at high level) required to produce them. Raising awareness in PRINCE2 is also useful.

3.2 PROJECT DEFINITION

| 1.1 Project Definition | The organisation recognises projects and runs them differently from its ongoing business. Projects may run informally with no standard process or tracking system.

3.2.1 P2MM content

P2MM does not take account of KPA 1.1 Project Definition since the characteristics of a Level 1 organisation mean that 'projects may run informally with **no standard process** or tracking system'. Instead, P2MM refers to the project management elements of P3M3. As Project Definition is an essential building block for implementing any project management capability, extracts from P3M3 are included here.

Purpose

The purpose of Project Definition is to gain a common and agreed understanding within an organisation that it conducts discrete projects, and that these projects are explicitly recognised. In defining projects the organisation should identify some project objectives. A project should also be managed i.e. subject to at least some management activities, including activity identification. A project is also likely to have some form of project lifecycle, which may be of benefit in high level planning.

Key Practices

Each project should have agreed objectives and be given the necessary resources to achieve those objectives.

The organisation should recognise the projects it is undertaking.

Each Project Manager should be able to identify the key activities that must be carried out.

Outline Project Plans are drawn up to distinguish project phases and/or stages.

Any changes in project requirements should be recognised.

3.2.2 Guidance

What does this KPA mean?

PRINCE2 states that 'A project, by its nature, is a temporary structure, created to achieve a specified business benefit or objective. When the work has been completed, the project is disbanded'.

This definition neatly captures why many organisations struggle with projects: they are undertaken *in addition* to your business-as-usual operations. The first step in gaining maturity in project management is to recognise what constitutes a project and what does not. This in turn means appreciating that project management is different from operations management or line management.

Having gained an understanding of what constitutes a project and what does not, it is important to identify which projects are under way in your organisation.

Why is this KPA necessary?

Because, what is unknown, cannot be managed!

Without an understanding of what projects your organisation has, there is likely to be confusion between operational activities and project activities. Some projects may start by stealth (the classic 'pet project'); others may grow so large such that they become departments in their own right. Such blurring makes it difficult (or impossible) to measure the effectiveness of one project compared with another because project costs will be hidden across the organisation's operational expenditure. In addition, it will not be possible to measure improvements in project management performance.

Understanding the type of projects you have is also an important step in identifying where best to invest. For example, you might have 60 live projects but if only 20% of these account for most of your expenditure you should consider what these 12 projects have in common (e.g. capital projects) and whether you can tackle those types of project first? It might be, however, that a different 20% of the projects will reap most of the benefits, so consider if these should be the focus of your attention? Or it might be that in analysing your list of projects you recognise commonality in the ones that tend to be late (IT projects or marketing projects?), so these might warrant greater focus.

In order to improve your understanding of your portfolio of projects you need to have some knowledge of the objective and scope of each as well as an appreciation of their current status and expected completion date.

How can this KPA be implemented?

It would be easy to say 'just set up a register', but before doing so you need to give some thought to the following:

- What are the boundaries of your organisation (does it include all departments, or just those in one country for example)?
- Is it more practical to have one register per department and only aggregate those projects that are over a certain size or that hit certain triggers? Or should the corporate register include only cross-functional projects?
- What constitutes a project and what sort of projects should be included in the register (e.g. customer projects, internal projects, subcontracted work, projects above a minimum budget, quantity of resource or timescale)?
- Who will maintain the register?
- How do you handle non-compliance?
- What information do you want to include on the register?

The answer to the last question could include the purpose of the project, agreed objectives, start/finish dates, approved budgets, project status, the Project Manager assigned and the business owner for each project. This in turn may require you to define the documentation requirements for each project. At this level of maturity this does not have to be 100% aligned to the suite of PRINCE2 management products, but it would help to accelerate maturity to introduce a few. (Be aware that distributing a set of 30+ templates at this stage of maturity is likely to be counter-productive.) Setting a policy for all projects to have a Project Brief, an Issue Log, and a Risk Log will vastly improve your projects.

The next step is to ensure that you appoint Project Managers to manage your projects, rather than subject experts or team leaders for example. This may require you to hire or train suitable Project Managers. Before recruiting externally, don't forget that there may be people in your organisation who were Project Managers with a previous employer and who would welcome the opportunity to get back into project management. Carrying out a skills assessment of your current employees (through a simple questionnaire) will help you to ascertain the level of project management experience within your organisation already. The level of project management skill expected of a Level 1 organisation is such that Project Managers are able to define the objectives and scope of a project and then break it down into manageable tasks in order to identify the resources required.

You should now be in a position to populate the Project Register for the first time. It may require some chasing and cajoling, however, to capture all the ongoing projects in your organisation and you may still find that the odd (pet) project remains below your radar. Setting a higher threshold to start with to create a short list and lowering the threshold later to produce a more complete list, will ease the task.

It is very likely that the first Project Register will highlight several anomalies. Senior management should review these anomalies to evaluate merging, closing, postponing or bringing forward some of the projects on the list. Remember, cancelling projects that can no longer be justified is a sign of maturity, not a sign of failure.

Finally, now that you have a Project Register you need to establish a mechanism to keep it up-to-date.

3.2.3 Examples

Stockport Metropolitan Borough Council

Stockport Metropolitan Council implemented PRINCE2 in a two-stage approach:

Stage 1 – establish the method

Stage 2 – embed the method

The first stage involved developing a Stockport-specific method (including a handbook, templates, and use of the intranet) and providing training (from top to bottom). The first stage was very successful with lots of anecdotal evidence of the method becoming 'the way' projects are run. However, as part of the 'embed the method' stage, participants recognised that they would benefit from a Project Register. The purpose of the central register is to avoid duplication of projects, assist the sharing of good practice and lessons learned and enable project progress to be incorporated into the council's performance management framework. Jo Lane, from Stockport's

Organisational and Learning Development department commented, 'The register is an important step. It lets people know that the council cares about the projects it runs'. Jo also provides a cautionary note, 'It is best to start small by defining the criteria of projects that need to be on the register such that only the largest, most important, or most complex projects are tracked. As the register gets more use the criteria can be expanded to increase the coverage of council projects being tracked'.

A supplier organisation

A supplier organisation was struggling with its sales performance. Faced with falling revenues and lower win ratios a number of managers within the organisation initiated improvement tasks to improve sales. There were initiatives to hire professional Bid Managers, to train Project Managers to become Bid Managers, to implement a Customer Relationship Management (CRM) system, to implement a new sales methodology, to change the way sales commission was calculated, and to train Account Managers in consultative selling techniques, to name but a few.

As this organisation did not have a Project Register, most of these projects were being managed in isolation until an announcement concerning one of the projects came to the attention of a second Project Manager. It transpired that aspects of the two projects were actually detrimental to each other. This prompted an investigation to uncover other sales performance-related projects. No fewer than 14 such projects came to light, involving more than 40 people and with combined budgets in excess of £1 million.

A project amnesty was held: all managers publicly declared their initiatives to enable the effective planning of a single, coherent set of projects. The majority of the projects were cancelled or postponed, the rest were re-shaped so that they would complement each other.

Key lessons learned from this organisation are:

- The benefits promised by each of the projects were very similar. If they had all come true then sales would have been unmanageable. In reality, the organisation was double-counting benefits.
- Some projects were un-doing or contradicting the work of others, for example, the bid management training would need to be re-run once the new sales method was implemented.
- The quantity of changes being implemented was reducing the number of 'sales days' spent with customers; probably contributing to the downward performance that the projects were trying to address.
- Project budgets were being taken from operational budgets, meaning that the true cost of the set of initiatives was not visible.

Level 2 maturity

4

4 Level 2 maturity

4.1 THE LEVEL 2 ORGANISATION

The Level 2 organisation is typified by having islands of good practice. Some projects will be very well managed, applying PRINCE2 appropriately and to good effect. However, there may be some projects using PRINCE in Name Only (PINO) or applying the method in an overly prescriptive way. There may be a company standard for PRINCE2 templates but it is just as likely that templates are copied from one project to the next. Some tools may be used in the Level 2 organisation, but it is likely that they have been adopted on a per project or per department basis.

To progress from this level:

- Projects should apply the PRINCE2 process model (Directing, Initiating, Controlling, Closing, etc.).
- Projects should have a Business Case to justify initiating and continuing the project.

- Clear descriptions of the roles and responsibilities for project participants should be provided. The roles should include a Project Board (with both customer and supplier representation) accountable for the project outcomes, a Project Manager who is singularly responsible for day-to-day project management, and a Project Support Team in keeping with the needs of the project.
- A product-based approach to planning is used to underpin the activities and resources required.
- Risks to a successful outcome for the project must be identified, quantified and managed.
- Project progress should be monitored so that management can make decisions on corrective actions should the project deviate from its agreed plan.
- Mechanisms should be in place to manage the quality of the project's deliverables (products) such that management has confidence that they will be 'fit for purpose' when handed over to the users.

Figure 4.1 Level 2 organisation

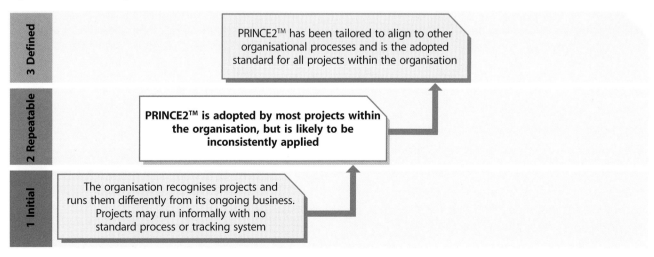

■ The project should recognise that requirements and plans will change as the project progresses. There needs to be a mechanism to control such changes to ensure that the desired outcomes can still be achieved within acceptable cost, time and risk constraints. The integrity of both management products and specialist products should be maintained through effective configuration management.

4.2 DIRECTING A PROJECT

> **2.1 Directing a Project**

PRINCE2™ is adopted by most projects within the organisation, but is likely to be inconsistently applied.

4.2.1 P2MM content

Purpose

The purpose of Directing a Project is to ensure that the Project Board exercises overall control over the project and takes responsibility for key decisions.

Key Practices

The Project Board manages by exception.

The Project Board fulfils its key responsibilities of:

■ Providing overall direction and decision-making
■ Committing appropriate resources to the project.

The Project Board authorises the Initiation Stage based on the Project Brief, and commits resources to the approved Initiation Stage Plan.

The Project Board authorises the project based on its fit with the business strategies as defined in the PID, and commits resources to the Next Stage Plan.

The Project Board undertakes End Stage Assessments to approve the work to date and provides authority to proceed to the next stage.

The Project Board monitors progress via Highlight Reports and provides ad hoc direction to the Project Manager.

The Project Board confirms Project Closure based on the End Project Report.

4.2.2 Guidance

What does this KPA mean?

Senior Managers are busy people. They cannot afford to be highly involved in every project for which they are responsible. They need to delegate the day-to-day management of a project, but ensure they have mechanisms in place to enable them to take the key decisions required of them. They must remain ultimately accountable. Senior Managers must also provide leadership and direction to ensure that each project remains aligned to the organisation's strategic aims.

Why is this KPA necessary?

The Project Board is the guiding coalition that is required to support and direct the project. As with company boards, if the composition of the Project Board is deficient then the project is likely to struggle. If the Project Board is embroiled in in-fighting the project is almost certainly doomed. Appointing the right Project Board is probably the single most important aspect of ensuring a good project.

The Project Executive needs to be able to exercise a balanced view on behalf of the wider organisation. The Senior User(s) must be able to make decisions on behalf of those groups who will use or gain benefit from the products when the project is completed. The Senior Supplier(s) must be able to make decisions on behalf of the organisation providing the expertise or resources to produce the products.

Tensions between Project Boards and Project Managers are unfortunately common. Some Senior Managers may bully the Project Manager into proceeding with an insufficient budget. Some Project Managers may disguise the real status or value of a project and can gain stakeholder support by producing good-looking reports and presenting them convincingly. Project Board members need to adopt a balanced approach when considering overruns, overspend, under-performance or informal changes and avoid having to micromanage the project themselves.

To gain such a balance the Project Board needs to allow the Project Manager to manage by exception. This is achieved through:

- Authorising the project to be initiated based on an outline Business Case (PRINCE2 Process DP1).
- Authorising the project to start based on a detailed Business Case supported by appropriate plans and controls (PRINCE2 Process DP2).
- Authorising the next stage of a project given satisfactory performance of the previous stage and an updated Business Case that justifies the project continuance (PRINCE2 Process DP3).
- Providing ad hoc advice and guidance to the Project Manager should the project forecast a breach in tolerance or should external influences need to be factored into the project (PRINCE2 Process DP4). This advice can be given by email, phone or in a meeting, but be careful not to reduce the value of other controls such as tolerance, Highlight Reports, and Exception Reports for example.
- Satisfying themselves that the project is being managed appropriately by establishing project assurance mechanisms (see also section 4.7).
- Confirming that the project has delivered the expected outputs, that those outputs are able to generate the outcomes defined in the Business Case, that the users

are ready to accept and support the products and that lessons learned have been captured and acted upon (PRINCE2 Process DP5).

Such practices are a part of good project governance, but some organisations may need to demonstrate that they are meeting legislative or regulatory requirements (e.g. Sarbanes-Oxley, Combined Code, or Code of Governance Standards for Public Services). Maturity in this Key Process Area provides a foundation for good project governance.

How can this KPA be implemented?

Gaining maturity in this KPA is about ensuring that Project Board members:

1 Are **capable** (skill and experience) of meeting their responsibilities for the project
2 Have suitable **authority** within their respective organisations to make decisions relating to the project
3 Have the **availability** to be able to commit sufficient time to the project.

The first of these points primarily relates to training for Senior Managers. There are three approaches here. The first is to provide Project Board training as part of a structured training programme (KPA 3.3). The second is to provide orientation training for first-time Project Board members (KPA 2.6). The third is to undertake a combination of the two. Senior management training should focus on establishing effective Project Boards using PRINCE2, covering their duties and the relationship with the Project Manager, rather than a PRINCE2 overview.

The second of these points can be achieved through aligning project accountabilities with an individual's job responsibility. Consider how the success of this project will be dependent on an individual's achievement of his/her personal objectives. In central Government for example all major projects must have a Senior Responsible Owner (SRO) appointed. The SRO's project responsibilities must be explicitly included in their personal objectives. In this way, the SRO is singularly accountable within the organisation for the success of the project (and in this context undertakes the role of the Project Executive).

Some organisations may already have an authority matrix showing the level of management authorised to make different levels of decision. Indeed, the Combined Code requires that UK-listed companies define the types of decisions to be taken by the board and those that can be delegated to management (a schedule of matters reserved).

The third point is about being realistic. The time required of the Project Board members is likely to be an important consideration. The complexity and visibility of the project and the proximity of key events in the project lifecycle will have a bearing on the investment that the Project Board members will have to commit to in terms of their time. Bear in mind that each Project Board member's level of participation is not likely to be uniform across the project. If the Senior Manager is unable to commit the necessary time, then either authority needs to be delegated to another board member (whilst ensuring points 1 and 2 are still valid), or to the Project Manager where appropriate (but be clear on the tolerances to trigger exceptions), or the continuation of the project should be questioned.

The structure, specific responsibilities and the mechanics of the Project Board should be defined in the PID. Be careful to avoid simply copying generic duties from the PRINCE2 manual: They should be specific.

Other implementation tactics can also include:

- Establishing a Project Register that identifies the owner for each project (KPA 1.1)
- Defining project and stage tolerances to enable management by exception (KPA 2.3)
- Aligning stop/go reviews (requiring projects to justify their continuation) to the project lifecycle (KPA 3.4).

4.2.3 Examples

A retail organisation

A UK retail organisation was implementing an electronic point of sale (EPOS) system across 36 of its convenience stores. The project comprised buying a bespoke application from a supplier in Scandinavia, integrating the system with in-store systems, HQ financial ledgers, HQ procurement and warehousing systems and providing training.

The project was forecast to take one year and on its third birthday the forecast timeline was still one year. The organisation decided to hire a professional Project Manager to help complete the project.

The project involved the IT Department, the Finance Department, Merchandising and Operations (which included the Store Managers). Because the principal driver behind the project was to achieve better deals from the manufacturers and wholesalers, by capturing data on the relationship between promotions and sales, the Head of Merchandising adopted the role of Project Executive. The IT Department provided most of the resources, Operations was affected the most as a result of changes to in-store practices, and the Finance Department was the gate-keeper deciding whether the EPOS system would be allowed to link to the financial ledgers.

The Project Manager applied PRINCE2 Project Board principles and recommended that:

- The Head of IT should be the Senior Supplier
- The Head of Merchandising, Head of Finance and Head of Operations should be the Senior Users as their departments would all benefit from a successful outcome of the project
- The Chief Executive Officer (CEO) should be the Project Executive.

The CEO was required to take on the role of Project Executive because none of the other candidates could wield sufficient authority over all the departments involved. The CEO didn't need much persuading to accept the role and commit time to the project once the Project Manager had highlighted the sunk costs and the risks of not completing the project. The project was completed within a year.

4.3 INITIATING A PROJECT

```
  2.2
Initiating a
 Project
```

PRINCE2™ is adopted by most projects within the organisation, but is likely to be inconsistently applied.

4.3.1 P2MM content

Purpose

The purpose of Initiating a Project is to ensure that the project is well defined and that there is a sound basis for its management and the assessment of its overall success.

Key Practices

A Project Brief is produced and approved to provide a full and firm foundation for the initiation of the project.

The initiation stage is formally authorised, based on the Project Brief.

A PID is produced in line with the PRINCE2 standard:

- The project objectives and benefits are defined and understood
- The project scope is defined
- Project tolerance is defined
- Reporting procedures, contents and frequency are defined

- Stakeholders' interests are identified and the means of communicating with these stakeholders is defined by the Communications Plan.

Formal approval to proceed to the next stage is provided by the Project Board, based on the PID and the Next Stage Plan:

- The Project Board accepts accountability for the success of the project and commits the appropriate resources to the project
- The PID is approved by the Project Board prior to work commencing on specialist products.

4.3.2 Guidance

What does this KPA mean?

A project should only start once the acceptance criteria are agreed and understood. These include the objectives of the project, the timeframe, the budget, the quality standards applied, the participants, the controls, and the measurement of success.

Why is this KPA necessary?

Overlooking this step, often leads to the development of PINO projects. A frequent excuse for rushing or sidestepping the initiation activities is: 'the project had such tight deadlines, that we didn't have time to plan'. It can be demonstrated time and again that every day spent planning will save or gain as many days during project delivery.

It costs money to plan a project. Therefore there should be a plan for the initiation activities and authorisation should be sought in order to proceed with the plan.

Expectations are set in this stage so they need to be managed carefully. It is cheaper to change the requirements, scope or strategy at this point than during project delivery or post-project.

It is common for people to define solutions before defining the problem or opportunity. Implementing the solution can then become more important than addressing the problem or gaining the benefits that were originally sought. The initiation activities provide a last opportunity to check that the requirements are properly defined and that the solution addresses the requirements before significant expenditure begins.

The critical initiation activities include:

- Confirming the customer's quality expectation and acceptance criteria and determining the Project Quality Plan required to ensure that the products will be fit for purpose (i.e. what does success look like?)
- Planning the project in detail
- Re-assessing the risks
- Validating the Business Case
- Setting up controls (configuration management, change control, reporting, and tolerances etc.)
- Documenting the above in the PID.

How can this KPA be implemented?

Initiation activities take time when done properly, so the main advice for successful initiation is to ensure that the Project Board commits sufficient time and resources.

Other tactics may include:

- Using the checklists in Appendix D of the PRINCE2 manual to assess readiness to start a project
- Indicating the project status in the Project Register (KPA 1.1). Projects that have bypassed initiation are worthy of a healthcheck (KPA 3.5)

- Ensuring that Project Board members are trained in PRINCE2 and recognise the value of a controlled initiation (KPA 3.2)
- Establishing a project gateway mechanism (KPA 3.4) linked to other business processes, such as budget approval or resource allocation (this may need to be filtered so that it only applies to projects over a certain size, visibility or risk profile).

4.3.3 Examples

Stockport Metropolitan Borough Council

Stockport Metropolitan Borough Council's implementation of PRINCE2 centres on an approach to assess the complexity of a project and then define how much of PRINCE2 should be applied to appropriately manage it. The initial assessment not only defines the level of management appointed to the Project Board roles but also defines the level of rigour required in order to initiate the project. The more complex and important the project, the more rigour is required to gain approval to proceed.

4.4 CONTROLLING A STAGE

2.3
Controlling a
Stage

PRINCE2™ is adopted by most projects within the organisation, but is likely to be inconsistently applied.

4.4.1 P2MM content

> #### Purpose
>
> The purpose of Controlling a Stage is to ensure that the Project Manager exercises day-to-day management of the project and reviews progress at the end of each stage.

Key Practices

All work is allocated through the use of Work Packages.

Information on actual progress in terms of cost, time and quality is collected, via Checkpoint Reports, and is used to update Stage Plans on a regular basis.

Project Issues are captured in the Issues Log, examined and resolved on a regular basis.

Progress is reviewed against the Stage Plan on a regular basis to ensure that it is kept within agreed tolerances.

Highlight Reports are produced for the Project Board at agreed intervals and are circulated to other stakeholders as defined by the Communications Plan.

Corrective action is taken by the Project Manager where appropriate.

If it is forecast that a plan will deviate beyond agreed tolerances, an Exception Report is issued to the Project Board.

At the end of each stage, the Project Manager prepares an End Stage Report in preparation for the End Stage Assessment to sign off completed stages and give approval to proceed.

4.4.2 Guidance

What does this KPA mean?

The purpose of project control is to ensure that the project:

- Remains viable against its Business Case
- Is producing the required deliverables, which meet the defined quality criteria
- Is being carried out to schedule and in accordance with its resource and cost plans.

Why is this KPA necessary?

Up until this point the plans are only theoretical. This is where they become reality. This is where the money gets spent and the resources consumed. If this part of the project is poorly managed all the good work to date could be wasted.

Project management efficiency is gained through management by exception so that Project Board members do not need to have day-to-day involvement in the project. This means that they can oversee more than one project and do their day job as well. Having agreed the project scope and objectives, the Project Manager is empowered by the Project Board to manage each stage subject to it remaining within certain time, cost, quality and risk tolerances. Therefore, the Project Manager needs to exercise sufficient control in order to ensure that the project remains within those tolerances.

Just as the Project Board empowers the Project Manager, so the Project Manager should empower people or organisations working on the project to undertake the activities necessary to develop the products required within each stage. In PRINCE2 this is achieved through Work Packages. Control mechanisms must be in place to ensure that:

- Work only starts on products when authorised
- ssues or risks associated with the products are captured, reviewed, resolved or escalated
- The status of the stage's products is recorded (e.g. pending, in development, under review, complete)
- Work Package owners report progress
- The Project Manager consolidates Work Package progress and submits Highlight Reports to the Project Board
- Prior to moving on to the next stage, the current stage is reviewed (and compared against its plan) so that lessons can be learned and applied while the project is still in progress.

How can this KPA be implemented?

Establishing effective controls requires effective use of tolerance. Tolerances should be more specific at the stage level than at the project level. Don't be bullied into not defining tolerances or simply setting generic levels:

- If the tolerance is too narrow the Project Executive becomes a surrogate Project Manager (micromanaging the project)
- If the tolerance is too wide the Project Manager becomes a surrogate Project Executive (making all the decisions)
- If no tolerance is set the project tends to either extreme (i.e. the Project Manager may escalate everything or nothing).

Agreeing tolerance is only useful if the status of the project is monitored and progress reported against the tolerances that have been allowed (and exceptions follow the agreed exception process). This is principally about establishing good communication channels with Work Package owners and recording the project status in logs:

- Product Checklist
- Issue Log
- Risk Log
- Quality Log
- Daily Log.

Using standardised templates for Work Packages, logs and reports (Checkpoint Reports, Issue Logs, Highlight Reports, etc.) and explaining them at project initiation and as new people or organisations join the project, will make controlling the project more efficient.

Project work or PRINCE2 may be completely new to some people working on the project. Some form of orientation training on the methods and controls used by the project is recommended – a digest in 'business speak' can be very useful. Project Managers should not assume that people will read the PID/Stage Plans and will automatically know what to do.

PRINCE2 does not describe meetings, it describes stage assessments and checkpoints. The frequency and format of progress reviews should be determined according to the pace, scale, visibility and complexity of the project. The Project Manager may choose to use email, conference calls, a collaboration tool (dashboard), meetings or 'floor walking' as the means to review progress. Likewise, the Project Manager may choose to use checkpoint meetings or emails to authorise Work Packages.

4.4.3 Examples

Financial Services Authority (FSA)

The Regulatory Services Management Services Unit (MSU) within the FSA aims to be a centre of excellence for the delivery of professional services and knowledge sharing to its internal business stakeholders. The unit recognised that business demand was changing, and wanted to improve its capability to support the business to deliver change more effectively. MSU set up a project to adapt the internal services offered to better support business-initiated changes, without increasing costs. The unit initiated a PRINCE2 project and used KPAs to deliver the change on time, to budget and in line with the required quality standards.

The PRINCE2 approach was successful even though it was a relatively small project. For example:

- MSU did not have dedicated project resources so it defined the resource requirements and ring-fenced the time that staff would spend on project work from their other activities. This, with a clear definition of Work Packages, enabled the Project Manager to define and control how much resource to allocate to each work stream at each stage.

- MSU used Product Descriptions to detail each deliverable, as the quality criteria section was invaluable for detailed planning and delivery. Where issues arose, the board reviewed the Product Description to decide the balance between schedule and quality and to enable the project to deliver the right products on time and to quality.

- Weekly Checkpoint Reports to the Project Manager and fortnightly Highlight Reports to the board ensured that delivery was controlled. Issues were escalated and the Product Manager issued an Exception Report if agreed tolerances were exceeded. Delivery was monitored against the Project Stage Plan.

- The project was organised into three stages. End Stage Assessments allowed the board to check that the project objectives were being met and that the project deliverables were still aligned to the vision of the organisation. The End Stage Assessments included an approval decision point to allow the next stage to begin. Lessons learned were noted at the end of each stage and applied in the later stages and to other similar projects.

This approach meant that the Project Board and the Project Manager had appropriate control over the project deliverables and could focus on key issues and decision points when needed.

4.5 CLOSING A PROJECT

2.4
Closing a
Project

PRINCE2™ is adopted by most projects within the organisation, but is likely to be inconsistently applied.

4.5.1 P2MM content

Purpose

The purpose of Closing a Project is to ensure that:

- The project comes to an orderly close
- Unfinished business is formally documented and passed on
- Lessons are learned from the project.

Key Practices

The PID is examined to check the actual results against original expectations.

Documented confirmation is obtained from the customer that all acceptance criteria have been met.

An End Project Report is prepared by the Project Manager, evaluating the actual project results versus those envisaged in the Project Initiation Document.

The Project Manager prepares Follow-on Action Recommendations based on outstanding Project Issues and risks.

A Lessons Learned Report is prepared based on the Lessons Learned Log maintained during the project.

An End Project Notification is prepared to advise the host location that facilities and resources will no longer be required.

Management documents are archived.

4.5.2 Guidance

What does this KPA mean?

Remember that PRINCE2 states 'A project, by its nature, is a temporary structure, created to achieve a specified business benefit or objective. When the work has been completed, the project is disbanded'. It should also state that when the project objectives have been met the project team is disbanded.

Mechanisms are required to check that the project objectives have been met and then ensure that the 'temporary project organisation' hands over ownership of the products to the user organisation, reviews lessons learned, recommends improvements and returns resources.

Why is this KPA necessary?

The money is spent; the products are complete. The success of the project could still be in jeopardy, however, if it is not closed down properly:

- The project's products are unlikely to provide direct benefits but will enable benefits to be gained (for example, the products required to implement a Quality Management System might be a quality manual, a set of processes and some training, but the benefits will only start being accrued once the QMS is in use). A post-project plan is required, therefore, to ensure that the business owners are able to realise the benefits expected.
- Costs can overrun if projects are not closed in a controlled way. People may continue to book to the cost-centre that was set up for the project for example.
- It is necessary to check that the users are ready to take responsibility for the products.
- It is necessary to check that there are support structures in place for the new products.

- The Project Manager may be perceived to be the owner of any open issues and risks and may be plagued with support queries for many months (or years) post-project if they are not closed down or if ownership is not explicitly transferred.

Projects can be difficult to close because of the psyche of typical Project Managers. People become Project Managers because they like change. The closure part of a project principally revolves around the transition to business-as-usual operations and Project Managers tend not to want to be in this space for too long. Additionally, most Project Managers will have one eye on their next project and that may become more interesting to them than closing down the current project.

Projects that close prematurely also need a controlled close. Unfortunately, it is all too common for projects to be abandoned and the latent value created to be lost. A case in point is the UK's 'tilting' Advanced Passenger Train. Development started in the late 1960s and was abandoned in 1981. Although the project did not reach its goal, it did advance train technology enormously – but that was not fully exploited for the benefit of British Rail. Fourteen years later, 'tilting' trains manufactured in Italy were in service on the UK's West Coast Main Line from London to Glasgow!

How can this KPA be implemented?

As with initiation, closure activities take time when done properly. The main advice for successful project closure is to ensure that the Project Board commits sufficient time and resources.

Other tactics may include:

- Using the checklists in the PRINCE2 manual to assess readiness to close the project

- Indicating the project status in the Project Register (KPA 1.1). Projects that go straight to 'close' or linger in 'pending close' for several months are worthy of a healthcheck (KPA 3.5)
- Ensuring Project Board members are trained in PRINCE2 and recognise the value of a controlled closed (KPA 3.2)
- Establishing a project gateway mechanism (KPA 3.4) linked to other business processes, such as budget approval or resource allocation (this may need to be filtered so that it only applies to projects over a certain size, visibility or risk profile) so that money and resources can no longer be allocated to a project once it has closed.

4.5.3 Example

A telecoms company

The project group responsible for provisioning new services for clients has a 'ready for service' checklist built into its PRINCE2-derived project management method. It is a prerequisite for requesting project closure to have evidence that the customer is ready to accept the service and that the service organisation is ready to support and maintain the new service. The 'ready for service' assessment covers the good practices recommended by PRINCE2 (such as closure or transfer of issues and risks, a Post-Project Review, Configuration Audit, etc.) as well legislative and regulatory requirements. The importance of the closure requirements is impressed so much on the Project Managers that many of them include it as an agenda item at the kick-off meeting!

4.6 BUSINESS CASE

2.5 Business Case

PRINCE2™ is adopted by most projects within the organisation, but is likely to be inconsistently applied.

4.6.1 P2MM content

Purpose

The purpose of Business Case is to ensure that there is sufficient justification for undertaking and continuing with the project.

Key Practices

A Business Case is produced which documents the justification for the undertaking of the project based on the estimated cost of the development and implementation against the risks and the anticipated business benefits and savings to be gained.

The Business Case includes the minimum information as defined by PRINCE2; i.e. Reasons, Options, Benefits, Risks, Cost, Timescale, Investment Appraisal and Evaluation.

Costs are based on the Project Plan.

Benefits are stated in terms that can be measured in the post-project review.

Investment appraisal is undertaken.

The Executive of the Project Board accepts ownership of the project's Business Case.

4.6.2 Guidance

What does this KPA mean?

Put simply, every project must have a Business Case. A Business Case is a description of the reasons for the project. The Business Case should:

- Have ownership within the organisation
- Be used to justify initiating the project
- Be used to justify continuing the project
- Be reviewed when assessing the impact of any changes or risks
- Provide the basis on which the project is measured for success
- Provide a means to compare the value of one project with another (to aid investment decisions).

Why is this KPA necessary?

A project is inextricably linked to its Business Case – without a viable Business Case there should be no project. It drives the decision-making processes and is used continually to align the project's progress to the business objectives/benefits that have been agreed – the strategic fit. As such, once a project starts, the Business Case should be maintained to ensure the project remains justified.

Most organisations will have far more projects on their wish list than they can afford or have the capacity to manage. Therefore when making investment decisions it is important to ascertain what benefits can be gained, when, with what degree of risk and at what level of investment. Additionally, projects should be evaluated on how well they contribute to corporate objectives. Such analysis enables one project to be compared with another so that the organisation can choose to invest in the best set of projects. Assuming that Senior Managers within the organisation have their objectives aligned to corporate goals, a well-crafted Business Case demonstrating a project's contribution to corporate objectives will gain

much greater sponsorship and commitment than one that is not.

Projects with poorly defined Business Cases often lack the clarity of vision that is required to keep them focused on the end result – the outcomes that the organisation is expecting. When such projects are faced with changes or risks, the impact analysis tends to focus on completing on time or within budget rather than the impact on the benefits that are being sought. It can be easy to forget that completing the project is only a means to an end and not the end itself.

If, for whatever reason, the Business Case is no longer valid, the project should be stopped. Stopping a project because its revised Business Case proves unjustifiable is a positive contribution to your organisation and shouldn't be seen as failure. The funds and resources it releases can be invested in other more worthwhile projects. This can be tough to do, so it is important to consider the options for a premature close when initiating a project (particularly where contracts are involved).

Organisations that lack rigour in developing Business Cases find that projects proceed even where there are few real benefits or where the project has only tentative associations with business strategy. Again, tough decisions need to be made.

The quality and content of a project's Business Case should not be left to chance. Mature organisations systematically ensure that all projects have Business Cases and that the Business Cases contain consistent content, are reviewed regularly and form the basis of decision-making.

How can this KPA be implemented?

Ensuring that all projects have a Business Case can be achieved by way of policy, particularly if linked to how your organisation allocates budgets or resources.

Implementation tactics can also include:

- Establishing a Project Register that indicates the owner, version and approval status of the Business Case for each project (KPA 1.1)
- Ensuring that Project Board agendas are based on a review of the Business Case (KPA 2.1)
- Ensuring that risk assessments focus on the impact on the Business Case (KPA 2.8)
- Ensuring that changes are assessed for impact on the Business Case (KPA 2.11)
- Developing a Business Case template based on your organisation's accounting rules and that scores the project against key criteria in support of corporate objectives (KPA 3.2)
- Providing training on how to develop and review Business Cases (KPA 3.3) – including how to value 'enabler projects'.
  (Note: An enabler project is a project that does not yield a direct return on investment but enables other projects to do so. Many IT infrastructure projects are enabler projects.)

When developing a Business Case template consult your finance department to ensure that the investment appraisal includes the same metrics they use, such as net present value, internal rate of return, hurdle rates, pay-back period, etc.

It is important to ensure that the desired outcomes or benefits are described in a form that can be measured; otherwise it will be difficult to use the Business Case as a means to measure success. Each outcome should have one or more Key Performance Indicators (KPI) so that the organisation can test whether the expected outcome has been achieved.

For large projects, a stand-alone Business Case document is recommended (see the PRINCE2 manual Appendix A). This will ensure that the Project Board reviews remain focused on the Business Case rather than the project details. For smaller projects it may be more efficient to embed the Business Case within the PID.

4.6.3 Examples

EDF Energy

Within EDF Energy, the Business Case is supported by a number of associated documents that are used throughout the investment lifecycle to create an investment case:

- Financial Investment Spreadsheet – templates and other investment analysis tools and spreadsheets are used across the business to build the financial information that goes into the investment case
- Benefits Tracker – the tracker records benefits expected against three categories (a) financial, (b) resources and (c) the company's strategic goals. Each benefit is assigned a Benefit Owner who must report on any changes to a benefit at each review point
- RAID Log – the Risk/Assumption/Issues/Dependencies Log supports the financial calculation of risk, which must be used to show how sensitive the business benefit is to key risks
- Benefits Realisation Statement – once the project has been completed and the benefits have been accrued, the Sponsor (who acts as the Project Executive during project delivery) completes a statement showing the actual benefit compared with the expected benefit as stated in the Business Case.

The organisation reviews the viability of the Business Case at the end of each stage; the Project Manager is expected to confirm that the forecast benefit is still on track.

4.7 ORGANISATION

2.6
Organisation

PRINCE2™ is adopted by most projects within the organisation, but is likely to be inconsistently applied.

4.7.1 P2MM content

Purpose

The purpose of Organisation is to establish an appropriate Project Management Team for the project ensuring that resources with the skills and competencies necessary to perform the management activities are made available.

Key Practices

All members of the Project Management Team are:

- Aware of their roles and responsibilities
- Understand the processes and procedures used to undertake these responsibilities
- Are suitably qualified and experienced for their roles.

A Project Board is appointed to provide overall direction and management of the project:

- It represents, at managerial level, the business, user and supplier interests
- The Executive accepts ultimate accountability for the success of the project and commits financial resources
- The Senior User adequately represents all user areas and commits user resources
- The role of Senior Supplier is clearly defined and commits supplier resources
- Project Assurance roles are agreed to ensure adherence to the agreed processes, procedures, tools and standards.

A single Project Manager is appointed as the focus for day-to-day management of the project:

- Responsible for the project producing the required products, to the required standard of quality, within specified constraints of time and cost
- Responsible for the project delivering an outcome that is capable of achieving the defined benefits.

The Team Manager role is used where appropriate.

Project Support is put in place.

Job descriptions are agreed where appropriate, identifying specific responsibilities and the qualifications/experience required.

4.7.2 Guidance

What does this KPA mean?

Projects are a people thing. You can't have a project if you don't have any people involved. No amount of good planning or control will help if the people involved do not know what's expected of them or what to expect of others. PRINCE2 addresses such issues by defining typical responsibilities for specific project roles.

Project governance is achieved by separating out the responsibilities of directing, managing and implementation as embodied in the Project Board, Project Manager, Team Manager and project team roles, respectively.

PRINCE2 roles are also based around a customer/supplier environment. The organisation structure assumes that there will be a customer who will specify the desired outcome, make use of the outcome and probably pay for the project, and a (prime) supplier who will provide the resources and skills to create that outcome.

The Organisation KPA is about ensuring that roles are allocated to people who are best capable (in terms of skill and authority) and committed (i.e. available and interested) to carry out their responsibilities.

Why is this KPA necessary?

A project is a temporary organisation that is needed to produce a unique and predefined outcome to satisfy a business need. Because of this, projects have different structures and needs from line management.

Typically, a project is cross-functional. It may involve external customers and suppliers, and a mixture of full- and part-time resources. The management structures of the parties involved in the project are likely to be different – each with different priorities, objectives and interests to protect.

Successful projects require an explicit project organisation structure defining the roles and responsibilities of the various participants and the skills involved in and required by the project.

A project organisation structure is needed to unite the various parties in the common aims of the project, to enable project governance and effective decision-making (by reducing the burden on senior management without removing the control), and to clarify what is expected of each role/participant.

In 2006 The National Audit Office (NAO) analysed successful major IT projects to identify common factors leading to success. Their report, *Delivering Successful IT-Enabled Business Change*, acknowledges the importance of good organisation structure by citing the following as one of the 10 Key Success Factors.

> A clear decision making structure with agreed lines of accountability so that the right decisions are made swiftly and in line with business strategy.

Source – NAO *'Delivering Successful IT-Enabled Business Change'*[5]

How can this KPA be implemented?

Following the guidance in the PRINCE2 manual for the Starting Up a Project process and sub-processes SU1, SU2 and SU3, in particular, would ensure a good project organisation structure is designed and appointed. Avoid the temptation to circumvent the start-up and initiation steps within PRINCE2. These are the processes that save you the most time and money; cutting them down is a false economy.

Some projects with well-defined structures and plans still manage to fail because the people involved do not understand their responsibilities. It is crucial to verify that everyone understands their responsibilities and the level of commitment required to discharge their responsibilities according to the roles assigned to them. It is a good idea to check whether the people assigned project roles have had any PRINCE2 orientation training.

General PRINCE2 training (one- or half-day briefings) will help with this KPA.

It is particularly common for people assigned the Senior User role to be unfamiliar with PRINCE2. If this is the case, there are a number of choices:

■ Include a half-day briefing on PRINCE2 as part of the project kick-off for those people who are unfamiliar with it, with a particular focus on roles and responsibilities

■ The centre of excellence or project management office (PMO) can provide a one-to-one briefing on how PRINCE2 works, the role of the Project Board and the role of the Senior User

■ The Project Manager could try to provide the briefing in a less formal way (perhaps in the form of a stakeholder review, getting the Senior User to specify his/her definition of success, the method of reporting etc. and then negotiating what's required of the Senior User in exchange)

- The Senior User role could be reallocated to someone who is better able to perform the role
- Without sufficient sponsorship the project should not proceed.

It is recommended that the project organisation structure is assessed on an ongoing basis to ensure that it is functioning well. This can be achieved through project assurance (as part of this KPA and KPA 2.1) and Quality Assurance (KPA 3.5). Telltale signs that the organisation is not working include:

- Action, Issue and Risk Logs are either empty or only a few people have contributed to them
- The Project Manager is listed as the owner of nearly all the entries in the Action, Issue and Risk Logs
- Single-stage projects – stage reviews are considered an unnecessary overhead
- Infrequent Checkpoint and Highlight Reports
- Tolerance is poorly defined (if at all)
- Projects continue without exception plans even if tolerance has been exceeded
- Projects start with key documents still in draft (who needs a baseline anyway?).

4.7.3 Example

Establishing a Supplier Project Board

In a supplier organisation that uses projects to deliver customer solutions, the choice of who fulfils each of the roles on a Supplier Project Board needs to be considered in relation to their bonus scheme or other reward mechanisms. It is important to ensure that those people allocated to a given role have personal objectives that encourage them to act in the manner expected of the role. For this particular organisation, the reward mechanisms in use were:

- Sales orders
- Invoices
- Project margin
- Customer satisfaction results.

If we take the Senior User for example, the recommended reward mechanism to encourage the Senior User to behave as the customer advocate would be the customer satisfaction result (is it what you expected?), invoices (can we bill what we have done?) and sales orders (can we have another one?). These objectives clearly pass the power to the customer and therefore require the Senior User to represent the specific customer's interests above others.

If we take the Project Executive, the recommended reward mechanism for him/her could be customer satisfaction result (have we met our promises?), invoices (can we bill what we have done?) and project margin (what's our profitability?). The latter can be influenced by increasing the price/scope for a given project and/or by reducing the project costs therefore creating the balanced view.

Figure 4.2 Reward mechanisms for Supplier Project Boards

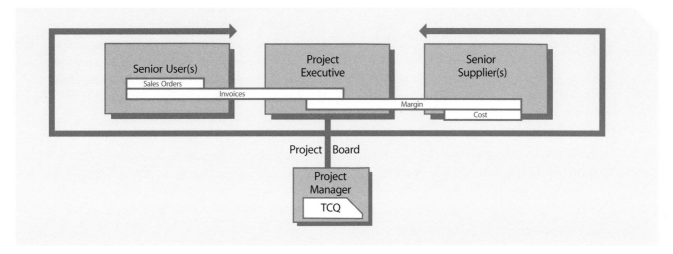

Taking the Senior Supplier, the recommended reward mechanism could be customer satisfaction result (does the solution work?), project margin (what's the profitability?), cost (have we delivered within budget?). The influence that the Senior Supplier has over the margin is to keep costs under control, keep changes/scope under control and to ensure that any designs are not over-engineered in the pre-sales phase.

Finally, if we look at the Project Manager, he/she clearly has an influence over customer satisfaction, but it is driven by the Project Manager's ability to deliver the project within time, cost and quality parameters.

Figure 4.2 shows that by overlaying the reward mechanisms on the Project Board a balanced structure emerges (assume everyone is allocated customer satisfaction result).

4.8   PLANS/PLANNING

PRINCE2™ is adopted by most projects within the organisation, but is likely to be inconsistently applied.

4.8.1 P2MM content

Purpose

The purpose of Plans/Planning is to establish credible plans for undertaking the required project and to underpin other project management activities, including the dissemination of planning information to stakeholders and other interested parties.

Key Practices

A Project Plan is created using the PRINCE2 Planning Process and an appropriate form of Product-Based Planning.

Strong emphasis is placed on identifying and specifying the products that the project is required to deliver and this provides a firm basis for defining the boundaries/scope of the project.

A Product Description is written for each significant product to ensure that it is understood, to describe how the product is to be presented and to define the quality expectations.

Where appropriate, Stage Plans, Team Plans and Exception Plans are also produced.

All plans contain, as a minimum, the following elements:

- Products, including prerequisites and quality requirements
- Activities needed to create and validate the quality of the products, plus the dependencies between products and any external dependencies
- Resources, and time needed for all activities
- Control Points, including tolerances
- Cost and time schedules.

All plans are approved and committed to by the relevant levels of the Project Management Team:

- For Project Plan and Stages Plans – Project Board and Project Manager
- For Team Plans – Project Manager and Team Manager.

4.8.2 Guidance

What does this KPA mean?

A plan is a document describing how, when and by whom a specified target or set of targets is to be achieved. A plan is a design of how identified targets for deliverables, timescales, costs and quality can be met.

Within PRINCE2, plans also include the descriptions of the project's deliverables – Product Descriptions. This means that the project must take a product-based approach to planning. Agreeing the project's products should precede defining the activities required to produce them and is therefore a prerequisite for scheduling.

Why is this KPA necessary?

Maturity in this KPA is essential for other Level 2 KPAs to be fully effective, in particular:

- Business Case (KPA 2.5) – A project's Business Case cannot be validated until planning is complete
- Organisation (KPA 2.6) – who needs to be involved depends on the content of the Project Plans
- Risk Management (KPA 2.8) – you can't forecast risk if you don't know what's already planned
- Controls (KPA 2.9) – ensuring the project keeps to the plan
- Quality Management (KPA 2.10) – doesn't work without Product Descriptions
- Configuration Management and Change Control (KPA 2.11) – needs a Product Breakdown Structure.

Effective planning identifies:

- The resources needed to achieve the targets within a timeframe
- The activities needed to ensure that quality can be built into the project's deliverables (outputs)
- The problems and risks associated with trying to achieve the targets and stay within the constraints

- Whether the targets are achievable.

Planning also:

- Provides the baseline against which progress can be monitored
- Communicates what needs to be done, how, when, by whom – and enables commitment to be gained from contributors and recipients.

Unfortunately few organisations spend enough time on planning, yet it is vital for a successful project. It is sadly common to see projects move to the next stage when the Stage Plan is not even drafted (sometimes the Project Manager may even be seeking sign-off on the last Stage Plan!).

How can this KPA be implemented?

The organisation needs to recognise that planning takes time and that it is time well invested. Therefore the single most effective technique for gaining maturity in this KPA is to allow time for planning. Resist the temptation to rush the project initiation and to start developing products before they are defined or agreed. Therefore this KPA is dependent on the effectiveness of Project Initiation (KPA 2.2), which is in turn dependent on having a supportive and competent Project Board (KPA 2.1).

Second only to 'allowing time' is ensuring that Project Managers are competent in Product-Based Planning (PBP) – this will almost certainly require some training (KPA 3.3) but will also require plenty of practice since PBP is a technique. It's a bit like learning mountain climbing, there's only so much theory that can be learned (education) before the techniques are honed through practice.

Most planning tools available on the desktop use a task-based approach to planning. That is, they focus on the activities (tasks) not the outputs (products). They can be seductive because of the ease of producing a Gantt chart.

But projects are not about tasks, they are about outputs. The tasks are simply the means to produce the output. When reviewing progress reports, the measure of progress is not how busy people are but how many of the products are complete.

Given that most planning tools encourage a task-based approach to planning, PBP is a planning paradigm few people are exposed to outside of their PRINCE2 training. Unfortunately the most training that many Project Managers get in PBP is about two hours on the day before they sit their PRINCE2 Practitioner exam – and at this point most people's attention is turned to exam preparation rather than learning a new technique.

Appointing a mentor to a Project Manager who is new to PBP is recommended to help him/her produce his/her first Product Breakdown Structure (PBS) and Product Flow Diagram (PFD). It is also useful during project initiation to brief or coach those people who will be producing or reviewing Product Descriptions. This could be in the form of a short workshop as part of the project kick-off, for example. It will significantly improve the clarity of the project's purpose, objectives, scope and deliverables (products).

Templates for planning documents will help, even if just to provide a checklist of things to consider. If in doubt, refer to the Product Outlines and Checklists in the PRINCE2 manual.

Planning tools can help, but are not essential. Level 2 maturity can be achieved using the tools on your desktop – a word processor, spreadsheet or a charting tool (e.g. MS Visio). Enterprise planning tools do improve efficiency, consistency and accuracy, but only if people are competent planners in the first place. There are now a number of planning tools that support a product-based approach, which help overcome the issues identified earlier in this chapter.

4.8.3 Example

Sun Microsystems Inc.

Sun's professional services group exists to help clients implement and gain benefit from their IT solutions. Most of the company's project work centres on the implementation of Sun hardware and software. Unsurprisingly, Sun naturally takes a product-based view of managing projects.

To reduce planning effort, Sun developed a library of Product Descriptions not only of management products but of the company's specialist products too. The library of Product Descriptions for specialist products includes pre-approved configurations of hardware and software products. As new or variant configurations are implemented the new or variant Product Description is added to the library, thus ensuring its currency.

Consultants and Project Managers can assemble solutions using the Product Description library quickly and with confidence, knowing that the Product Descriptions are based on proven implementations.

4.9 MANAGEMENT OF RISK

> 2.8
> Management
> of Risk

PRINCE2™ is adopted by most projects within the organisation, but is likely to be inconsistently applied.

4.9.1 P2MM content

> **Purpose**
>
> The purpose of Management of Risk is to identify, analyse, minimise or control the possible adverse effects associated with risks that materialise prior to, or during, the conduct of a project.

> **Key Practices**
>
> The Project Board and Project Manager agree the amount of risk they are prepared to tolerate, i.e. the risk tolerance.
>
> The responsibilities for the management of risk are agreed between the Project Board and Project Manager.
>
> An owner is identified for each risk, who should be the person best situated to monitor it.
>
> Risk analysis is undertaken, as a minimum during initiation and at the end of every stage, consisting of:
>
> - Identifying risks
> - Evaluating risks, taking into account impact, probability and proximity
> - Identifying suitable responses, i.e. prevention, reduction, transference, acceptance or contingency
> - Selecting responses.
>
> Risk Management is undertaken on an ongoing basis, consisting of:
>
> - Planning and resourcing selected responses
> - Monitoring and reporting
> - A Risk Log is maintained to hold information about risk, risk analysis, countermeasures and status.

4.9.2 Guidance

What does this KPA mean?

Management of risk is systematic: it is not based on chance. It is about the identification, analysis and control of the key factors (or sensitivities) affecting the delivery of benefits as expressed in the Business Case. The key consideration to bear in mind is: 'Can this project be allowed to overrun in terms of cost, time, quality, or scope, etc., and if not, what should the project do to minimise either the likelihood of this happening, or the effect on the Business Case?'

Why is this KPA necessary?

A risk may be defined as 'uncertainty of outcome' or, put another way 'a future event, that should it happen will have an adverse (or maybe a positive) impact on your project'.

The impact could be in terms of time, cost, quality, scope or the benefits being sought. In all instances the impact on the Business Case should be considered, since an uneconomic Business Case means there is no justification for the project. Risk taking in projects is inevitable since projects are tools of change and change introduces uncertainty and hence risk.

The purpose of risk management is to provide a systematic way of managing the project's exposure to risk by taking action to keep exposure to an acceptable level in a cost-effective way. It involves establishing a method for risk identification and analysis, for determining mitigation strategies (proactive), contingency strategies (planned, reactive), implementing those strategies as required, monitoring identified risks and developing a strategy for dealing with other unforeseen events (unplanned, reactive).

How can this KPA be implemented?

A risk management process needs to be defined for the project, in the same way that there should be a planning process or a quality process. The content of the risk management process will vary depending on the technical, political and organisational complexity of the project. The risk management process specific to the project should be defined during Project Initiation (KPA 2.2) and documented in the PID. The OGC's Management of Risk6 provides comprehensive guidance on how to manage project risk.

The Project Manager should consider the following points when creating the process:

- Understand the client's risk appetite and agree the level of risk tolerance permissible by the Project Board (KPA 2.1)
- Agree and publish the steps in the risk process (in the PID)
- Define the tools and techniques to be used in the project (in the PID)
- Allocate specific owners to all the various parts of the risk process and define their roles and responsibilities
- Use a predefined template (Risk Log) to capture risks (KPA 2.9)
- Use warning flags to indicate areas of concern and consider how to add this data into the Highlight Report (KPA 2.3)
- Embed risk reporting into Checkpoint, Highlight, End Stage and End Project Reports
- Embed risk assessment into Change Control (KPA 2.11) and exception handling processes (KPA 2.3)
- Define how the Project Board will deal with any risks that have been escalated
- Understand how risks affect the business benefits from the project, making sure that there are no missed opportunities to reap extra rewards (KPA 2.5).

Once you have a process and some techniques to apply, you can begin analysing the risks on the project. The Risk Analysis components of Identify the risks, Evaluate the risks, Identify suitable responses to risk and Select, will enable you to populate the Risk Log (see Chapter 17 of the PRINCE2 Manual for more details). Consider using some of the following techniques:

- Use a Risk Checklist when assessing client requirements
- Use a Risk Breakdown Structure to group risks into specific risk categories (see Appendix C of the PRINCE2 manual for an example)

- Use a risk scorecard to determine how much project management overhead to apply
- Apply Ishikawa root-cause-analysis techniques (sometimes called a fishbone diagram) to assess risks and mitigation options
- Calculate a risk budget for (complex) assignments based on quantitative as well as qualitative analysis of risks.

4.9.3 Examples

Risk management process

Figure 4.3 depicts the project's risk process as a 'swim-lane' diagram, which can be included in the PID.

Defining risk categories

Table 4.1. illustrates a typical example of a risk category matrix.

Table 4.1 Example probability impact table

	Low probability	Medium probability	High probability
High impact	C	B	A
Medium impact	D	C	B
Low impact	E	D	C

To ensure that risks gain the appropriate level of visibility and ownership you will need to define:

- What you mean by high, medium and low probability
- What you mean by high, medium and low impact (see Table 4.2)
- What you do with the A, B, C, D, E resulting categorisation (see Table 4.3).

Table 4.2 defines the health and safety risks associated with a given project and the financial impact they represent. You could add other columns (e.g. time, benefits, scope).

Table 4.2 Example impact definitions

Impact	Description	Financial impact
Low	First aid treatment or medical treatment required, but no lasting disability	< £100,000
Medium	Injuries leading to permanent disability	£100,000 – £1 million
High	Death	> £1 million

Table 4.3 Example category definitions

Category	Definition	Action
A	Risk response identified and approved for implementation	Terminate, treat or transfer
	Weekly status reporting to Project Board	
B	Risk response identified and approved for implementation	Terminate, treat or transfer
	Weekly monitoring of risk triggers	
C	Risk response identified but not implemented	Tolerate
	Weekly monitoring of risk triggers	Tolerate
D	Risk triggers monitored	Tolerate
E	Ignore	Tolerate

Figure 4.3 Example project risk process

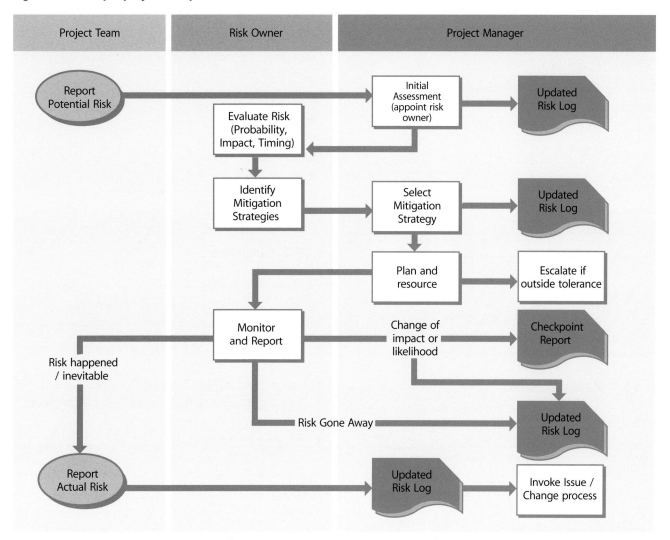

The numerical approach shown in Table 4.4 involves a simple scoring matrix for probability and impact (1-9 on each axis for example). Either plot the results or simply multiply the axes to obtain the worst-case risk from an ordered set.

Table 4.4 Example numerical approach to ranking risks

Risk ID	Probability	Impact	Weight
R001	7	7	49
R006	8	4	32
R003	2	9	18
R013	4	4	16
R007	4	3	12

4.10 CONTROLS

2.9 Controls

PRINCE2™ is adopted by most projects within the organisation, but is likely to be inconsistently applied.

4.10.1 P2MM content

Purpose

The purpose of Controls is to provide adequate visibility into actual project progress so that management can take effective action if the project's performance deviates significantly from the Project Plans.

Key Practices

The Project Board exercises control by way of:

- Project Initiation (during which the Project Plan is produced and the use of Stages and Tolerances are agreed with the Project Manager)
- End Stage Assessments
- Highlight Reports

- Exception Reports
- Exception Assessments.

The Project Manager exercises control by the appropriate use of PRINCE2 management products, for example:

- Stage Plans
- Product Descriptions
- Work Packages
- Checkpoint Reports
- Quality Log
- Daily Log
- Issue and Risk Logs.

4.10.2 Guidance

What does this KPA mean?

Controls ensure that, for each level of the Project Management Team, the next level up of management can:

- Monitor progress and compare achievement against the plan
- Review plans and options against future situations
- Detect problems, identify risks and initiate corrective action
- Authorise further work.

Why is this KPA necessary?

Without Controls there is no guarantee that the project will deliver what is expected of it. It is not surprising therefore that the world's most popular project management method is fundamentally about project control (PRINCE® stands for PRojects IN **Controlled** Environments).

Projects are based on temporary organisations that have different structures and needs from line management. Therefore the project will require control mechanisms specific to the structure of the organisations involved, which will be different from those embedded within a line management structure.

Projects involve an element of uniqueness, which requires them to be managed in a different way from existing operations. Therefore the project will require control mechanisms specific to the nature of the undertaking, which will be different from those embedded within operational processes.

With an ever-increasing focus on governance, each layer of management should ensure that appropriate controls are in place to ensure that delegated powers are used appropriately without the need for micromanagement.

How can this KPA be implemented?

At the heart of project control is the PID. Despite its name, the Project **Initiation** Document is used to control the project throughout its life, not just during initiation.

The PID contains the who, what, where, why, when and how of the project. Depending on the size and complexity of the project, the PID may reference many other documents, such as a Project Plan, or it may be a composite of the many project documents recommended by PRINCE2. In either case it is the principal project document and it defines how the project will be controlled. It should be the first point of reference for anyone involved with the project.

Do not assume that people working on the project will be familiar with PRINCE2 controls. It is worthwhile providing an overview of the Controls as part of a project kick-off meeting. Avoid the temptation to simply issue a PID asking people to read it, because, chances are, they won't.

Aligning the project's End Stage Assessments with company approval and reporting processes is a worthwhile tactic if this has not been done at the organisation level (KPA 3.2).

Establishing maturity in Directing a Project (KPA 2.1), Initiating a Project (KPA 2.2), Controlling a Stage (KPA 2.3) and Closing a Project (KPA 2.4) will ensure maturity in this KPA. The repetition of the controls from those four KPAs might seem strange but it is analogous to the PRINCE2 manual itself in that the Controls component is a summary of the controls embedded in the PRINCE2 processes. This KPA provides the overview of how controls operate across the management layers, which is not as easy to review when looking at the controls within each of the four KPAs listed above separately.

4.10.3 Examples

Investment bank

Operating in a regulated industry, the bank already had controls in place with respect to authority levels, risk management requirements and reporting. The early stages of the bank's adoption of PRINCE2 as its project management method involved mapping PRINCE2 controls to existing company controls. This resulted in a matrix being produced to illustrate the 'levels of ceremony' required for the different types of project. The tolerances defined by the 'levels of ceremony' could then be incorporated in the PID.

4.11 QUALITY MANAGEMENT

PRINCE2™ is adopted by most projects within the organisation, but is likely to be inconsistently applied.

4.11.1 P2MM content

Purpose

The purpose of Quality Management is to provide management with confidence that the project processes are resulting in products of a suitable level of quality.

Key Practices

Customer's quality expectations and acceptance criteria are defined and agreed with the Senior User and are captured in the Project Quality Plan.

A Project Quality Plan is produced which defines, in general terms, how the project will meet the customer's quality expectations.

Each Stage Plan specifies in detail the required quality activities and resources, with the detailed quality criteria shown in the Product Descriptions.

The quality of products is verified against quality criteria as part of Executing Work Packages, and the results of these quality controls are recorded in the Quality Log.

All necessary stakeholders are involved in quality control activities.

Identified problems with quality are raised as Project Issues, captured, examined and if necessary escalated to the Project Board.

4.11.2 Guidance

What does this KPA mean?

Quality is a question of identifying what it is about the project's products (deliverables or service) that makes them 'fit for the purpose' of satisfying customer requirements. Projects should not rely on implied needs. Quality Management is the process of ensuring that the quality expected by the customer is achieved. It involves:

- Capturing and verifying the customer's quality expectations (CQE)
- Transforming the CQE into acceptance criteria for the requirement
- Identifying the products that are required to meet the acceptance criteria

- Defining each product's purpose, quality criteria (fitness for purpose measures) and quality checking method
- Agreeing that the Product Descriptions accurately reflect the customer's requirements
- Verifying that all products have been completed, that quality checks have been carried out for each product and that the quality criteria is satisfied.

Why is this KPA necessary?

Quality in a project environment is different from what many people may be familiar with in an operational environment (e.g. an ISO 9000 Quality Management System). Therefore, the processes that the project will use to ensure customer requirements are fulfilled need consideration and definition.

A project can be subject to disputes if there is no explicit understanding of the criteria against which each product will be accepted by the users. Such disputes will have a negative impact on the Business Case as a result of:

- Additional management and user intervention
- Re-work
- Extra work
- Project delays
- Delayed benefits.

Additionally, if the customer/supplier environment is a commercial relationship (i.e. a buyer/seller relationship) such disputes are likely to have a detrimental affect on the relationship between the organisations.

Products are much cheaper to change when they are in the design stage than when they are in use. This is why the construction industry produces artists' impressions and architects' models when consulting with customers and stakeholders for civil engineering works. Whether using models or prototypes, the process of gaining customer approval of the design or description of the project's products is an important part of the quality management process.

Research by quality gurus such as Phil Crosby has shown that the cost of correction is many times that of prevention. For example, the infamous Millennium Bridge in London cost an original £18.2 million to build but had to be closed after just three days of use because of excessive swaying. Resonant vibrational modes are well understood in bridge designs, but lateral movement caused by pedestrians was not anticipated by the computational analysis of the bridge prior to construction. The cost of fixing the problem was about £5 million and the bridge reopened eight months later.

Finally, the cost of acceptance and the time required for acceptance is often overlooked. Without an understanding of the acceptance criteria it is not possible to define the quality checking method. If you have not specified the quality checking method it is not possible to define the cost and timescale for the project. In the software development industry it is not untypical for testing and acceptance to take longer than the time required for design and development. In the satellite communications industry, for example, it is typical to test satellite components 'to destruction'. That is, rather than testing that a product meets specifications for noise, vibration, temperature and dust thresholds, it will be tested several times to destruction to determine the lowest point at which the product fails. If the lowest result is above the required threshold then the product will pass. A component costing £200,000 to manufacture might be tested five times to destruction even though there might only be 10 items in use when it passes. The manufacturing cost for the project is 15 x £200,000 (£3 million), not 10 x £200,000 (£2 million)!

How can this KPA be implemented?

Product Descriptions form the nucleus of project quality. They are the basis on which products are defined before they are designed and developed. They are also the reference against which the products are assessed for conformity to requirements once they have been produced. Therefore it is essential that a product-based approach is taken when defining the project's deliverables (products) in order to avoid downstream disputes as to whether the project has met its requirements. Maturity in this KPA is dependent on maturity in Planning (KPA 2.7).

Project Quality starts during start-up when the outline requirements and scope of the project are defined. At this point it is important to understand the customer's (or users') quality expectations and if any top-level acceptance criteria can be agreed in order to help plan and define the project in more detail. By the end of project initiation these inputs will have shaped the set of required products and the Project Approach (for example, in an IT project the options could be to buy off-the-shelf systems or to develop a bespoke application in-house). Maturity in this KPA is dependent on maturity in Project Initiation (KPA 2.2).

It is also important to determine if and how any corporate quality requirements of those organisations involved will be incorporated into the project. If the supplier organisation is external it will almost certainly use different quality systems from the customer. Defining which policies, systems and standards will apply is important. These will influence the content of the Project Quality Plan and consequently the quality checking method for verifying conformity to requirements for each product.

Keeping an up-to-date Quality Log showing the status of planned and actual quality activities will provide management with confidence that the project's processes are resulting in products of a suitable level of quality.

Figure 4.4 Quality-related products

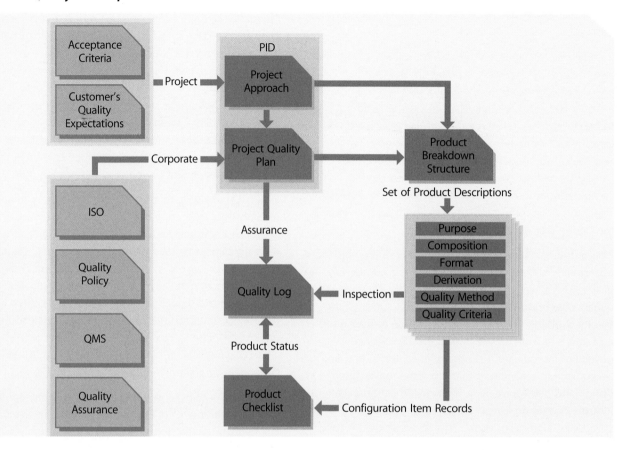

4.11.3 Examples

Extract from a Project Quality Plan

Figure 4.4 was incorporated in a Project Quality Plan to explain to those people working on the project who were unfamiliar with PRINCE2 how the various management products related with respect to gaining client acceptance for the project's products.

4.12 CONFIGURATION MANAGEMENT AND CHANGE CONTROL

2.11
Config Mgmt
and Change
Control

PRINCE2™ is adopted by most projects within the organisation, but is likely to be inconsistently applied.

4.12.1 P2MM content

Purpose

The purpose of Configuration Management and Change Control is to establish and maintain the integrity of the project documentation and specialist products throughout the life of the project, and to ensure that decisions on the implementation of changes are based on a sound assessment of the implications of such changes.

Key Practices

A Configuration Management Plan is produced which identifies how and by whom the project's products will be controlled and protected. This should identify the person with responsibility for undertaking the role of Configuration Librarian.

All products are uniquely identified and the relationships between products established.

All products are baselined following the successful completion of quality control:

- Products are submitted to the Configuration Librarian
- Where practical, master copies are retained and copies alone are issued.

Product records are kept up-to-date to enable accurate status accounting.

Configuration Audits are undertaken at the end of every stage.

All changes are dealt with as types of Project Issue and a record is maintained through the Issue Log.

The authority for approving or rejecting Project Issues is decided on by the Project Board during the initiation stage.

Members of the Project Board are involved in making decisions on Requests for Change where the Project Board members may be affected.

4.12.2 Guidance

What does this KPA mean?

Configuration Management is a discipline that gives an organisation precise control over its assets. The process includes planning, identification, control, status accounting and verification. Within the context of project management, the purpose of configuration management is to identify, track and protect the project's assets (i.e. its deliverables or products).

The purpose of change control is to establish a method of assessing the impact of potential changes, their importance and their cost and then gaining a judgement decision by management on whether or not to include them.

Why is this KPA necessary?

If more than one version of a product is created, then configuration management is required (it is not optional). Projects with poor configuration management can experience the following:

- People developing products to an out-of-date specification
- People unknowingly working on a product at the same time as someone else
- Defects that had been fixed reappearing in later versions
- All products may have to be recalled to fix a defect even though the defect is only present in a small number of products (i.e. a single batch of products).

Changes originate from external (customer) requests, project team suggestions, management decisions or Project Issues and risks. Change is, therefore, highly likely. Changes to specification or scope can potentially ruin any project unless they are carefully controlled. If the impact of a change is not checked against the Business Case for continued viability, then the project might continue even though there's no justification for it to do so.

How can this KPA be implemented?

If your organisation has a Quality Management System (QMS) that is ISO 9001 compliant then it will have processes in place for configuration management, change control and document management. If you have a QMS that is not ISO 9001 compliant, the chances are that it might have some aspects of configuration management, change control and documentation management included. In the first instance it is wise to find out what your organisation already has available to you and then look at how it can be applied to your projects. An existing QMS might have to be adapted for a project context since it is likely to be focused around your business-as-usual operations. If possible, make the Configuration Management Plan a part of the Project Quality Plan – and keep it specific to the project. Avoid pasting in generic configuration management text because it will not be read. A Project Quality Plan that refers to company processes or international standards makes for a slim document and also reduces the degree of orientation training that people may require when joining a project.

The main consideration when defining a Configuration Management Plan is to decide at what level of product you wish to apply controls. Therefore, an initial step to configuration management planning is to uniquely tag (e.g. number) the products on the Product Breakdown Structure (PBS). Product Descriptions should be produced for those items that need to be controlled, together with an entry in the Product Checklist.

A fundamental principle for change management is the concept of a **baseline**. Without a baseline it is not possible to determine the starting point from which change will be measured. Without a baseline it is also highly likely that the project will end in some form of dispute as to whether the project has delivered its requirements. A baseline needs to be set for:

- Timescale
- Budget
- Scope
- Quality
- Benefit.

It is also important to map authority levels to types of change requests, so that decisions on changes can be made at the most appropriate level within the project organisation. This should be documented as part of the controls section of the PID.

4.12.3 Example

The PBS illustrated in Figure 4.5 was used to help define products for an organisation wishing to deploy PRINCE2. There was a worthy debate as to whether the PBS item 2.2.4 (Templates) should be broken down further. The considerations being:

- Should the organisation have a single Product Description covering all the templates required and refer to the Product Outlines in Appendix A of the PRINCE2 manual or should the organisation produce a Product Description per template.
- If the organisation sourced a set of templates designed and produced externally, would that change the level of configuration control required?
- Can some templates be derived from existing company templates and if so, do they require a specific design detailing how to incorporate specific company processes (e.g. the Business Case template to incorporate budget approval requirements)?

Figure 4.5 Example PBS

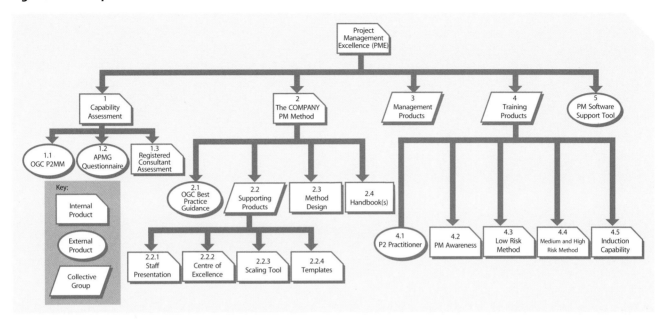

- Are there relationships between specific templates and other products in the project (e.g. the PID template and the Scaling Tool, 2.2.3)?
- Should templates have a version number and if so, should it be a version number for the entire set or a version for each template?

The level at which Configuration Items are managed corresponds directly with the Product Descriptions that should be produced. Generally, the greater the level of control, the more Product Descriptions are required. These take time to produce and maintain, so there will come a point when the value to be gained from exercising greater control does not justify the additional work.

Level 3 maturity

5

5 Level 3 maturity

5.1 THE LEVEL 3 ORGANISATION

For the Level 3 organisation, the question has moved on from 'Did the project deliver the desired outputs on time and within budget?' to 'Do **all** of our projects deliver the desired outputs on time and within budget and have the expected benefits been realised?' All projects within the organisation follow a standard approach based on PRINCE2 or are able to justify why they don't (and have the necessary approvals for non-compliance).

To fully meet the requirements of this level:

■ The organisation needs to establish ownership for project management as a core capability. The owner should review how well PRINCE2 is being applied and, at least annually, produce an improvement plan that is implemented and reviewed on an ongoing basis. Establishing a centre of excellence or project management office will help (refer to P3M3 for guidance as this is outside the scope of P2MM).

■ A company-specific project management handbook should be available containing policies on how PRINCE2 is applied to the organisation's various types of projects. The handbook will include standards for documentation, planning, estimating and use of project management tools. A common set of PRINCE2 templates will be available for all Project Managers to use. The templates are subject to change control and continuous improvement via lessons learned reviews.

■ Training in PRINCE2 and other project management competencies is no longer based on a generic approach but instead is specific to the needs of the role and is oriented towards the organisation's implementation of PRINCE2 as embodied in their handbook.

■ PRINCE2 is appropriately applied to each project according to the project's size, complexity and importance, with adequate resources being allocated for the project management activities – any deviation from PRINCE2 is documented.

Figure 5.1 Level 3 organisation

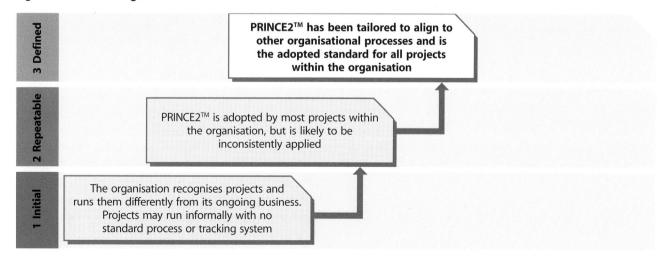

■ An assurance mechanism is in place to monitor the application of PRINCE2 to ensure that projects are able to deliver products that meet their quality criteria.

5.2   ORGANISATIONAL FOCUS

3.1 Organisational Focus

PRINCE2™ has been tailored to align to other organisational processes and is the adopted standard for all projects within the organisation.

5.2.1 P2MM content

Purpose

The purpose of Organisational Focus is to establish the organisational responsibility for the adoption of PRINCE2 with the aim of improving the organisation's overall project management capability.

Key Practices

There is a defined role within the organisation with the responsibility for coordinating the use of PRINCE2.

This role has the appropriate level of authority to mandate the use of PRINCE2 on all projects within the organisation.

Sufficient time/resource is made available to make this role effective and to provide support/mentoring to Project Managers and project teams.

Project Managers consistently apply the PRINCE2 method to help them produce the required project deliverables.

Data is collected to enable improvements to the use of PRINCE2 to be made.

The effectiveness of PRINCE2 is reviewed at least annually, with input from Project Board members.

Recommendations from these reviews are incorporated into an improvement plan that is implemented and reviewed on an ongoing basis.

5.2.2 Guidance

What does this KPA mean?

The adoption and continued use of PRINCE2 will change the way an organisation works and create a new culture. It should, therefore, be considered a change programme. There must be appropriate sponsorship for the implementation, adoption and improvement tranches of the programme. Roles and responsibilities for business change and ongoing ownership should be clearly defined.

An organisational focus is required to ensure that the implementation and continued use of PRINCE2 can be monitored to see whether the business benefits used to justify its adoption are being achieved.

Gaining ownership and sponsorship is the most critical step in implementing PRINCE2. Trying to implement PRINCE2 from the bottom up is likely to fail. It needs a top-down approach because it permeates the whole organisation. Ownership is also a prerequisite for establishing a continuous improvement capability.

Why is this KPA necessary?

There is more to implementing PRINCE2 than developing a handbook, some templates and sending a few people on some PRINCE2 training courses. The successful implementation and continued use of PRINCE2 requires a new culture to be established. Elements of PRINCE2 such as Project Boards, product-based plans, tolerance and exception management (to name a few) need to be institutionalised so that they become the norm for the organisation.

Many organisations make the mistake of treating the implementation of PRINCE2 as a destination: once they've arrived, they can tick the box. It is not a destination, however, it's a journey that will continue for as long as your organisation and the requirements of it continue to change.

Organisations typically give the task of implementing PRINCE2 to their most experienced Project Manager. There is nothing wrong with this approach; after all it is a project (even if it is part of a broader programme). The Project Manager is likely to be seen as the champion for PRINCE2 and can easily become the internal owner for PRINCE2 once the project has finished. Project Managers aren't generally interested in the maintenance of a method after rollout, however, as they like change. That's why they are good Project Managers. Once PRINCE2 has been successfully implemented, the Project Manager will very likely to want to move on to the organisation's next most challenging project. If you accept this as inevitable, then the team that will own and support PRINCE2 is likely to be different from the team that implements it.

Without ongoing ownership, focus and support, old habits will creep back in. A sign of maturity is an organisation that has processes, templates and tools beyond version 1 – they have been field-tested and updated based on data aggregated from lessons learned and project audits.

How can this KPA be implemented?

When organisations decide to implement PRINCE2, they have already made the decision that they wish to be P2MM Level 3. That is, that they want PRINCE2 to be consistently applied across all projects within the organisation. Therefore this KPA needs to be implemented as part of the wider initiative to implement PRINCE2 (see section 2.1).

Careful consideration of what the organisation will look like when PRINCE2 is implemented will help you design the implementation strategy:

- Who should own it? What does 'it' in fact mean?
- What ongoing infrastructure is required? For example:
  - A feedback mechanism on the handbook, templates, tools, etc. (e.g. a central issues log)
  - A repository and review mechanism for lessons learned
  - A change requests mechanism on the handbook, templates, tools, etc.
  - A release mechanism for updates to the handbook, templates, tools, etc.
  - A PMO to measure PRINCE2's adoption, use, and benefits
  - A PMO to provide advice and guidance
  - A training curriculum
  - A means to train new starters
  - A development path for Project Managers
  - An audit programme to assess compliance
  - Maintenance facilities for any support or automation tools used
  - A means to keep up-to-date with best practices (a centre of excellence?)
  - A pan-organisation project management community (conferences, show-and-tell sessions)
  - Newsletters, etc.

- How much will all that cost to implement? How much will it cost on an ongoing basis?
  - Additional headcount (PMO resources)
  - Training budgets
  - Software support contracts
  - Professional membership fees
  - Accreditation fees

- How do we know if it's working?
  - PMO too big, too small

- Linkage with satisfaction surveys (e.g. customers, staff, shareholders, stakeholders)
- Linkage with Key Performance Indicators (e.g. time to market, the percentage of project overspend, the percentage of project overrun).

It is critical that implementation is reviewed and improved otherwise people are likely to revert to old practices. A simple measure of maturity used by many auditors is how much of a management system moves beyond version 1.0 by its first anniversary! Section 2.1.4 describes the need to establish Key Performance Indicators during implementation as a means to provide a mechanism for ongoing improvement.

5.2.3 Example

EDF Energy

EDF Energy is one of the largest energy companies in the UK. It is divided into four branches. Figure 5.2 shows how the implementation project was structured to develop and roll out EDF Energy Project Way (EEPW), which is based on best practices from various internal and external sources as well as PRINCE2. Each branch nominated a sponsor to sit on the Project Board.

Portfolio Support Offices were established to support projects and ensure alignment to the governance and methodology of EEPW at branch level. There is now a central team responsible for the custodianship and future development of the EEPW processes and methodology.

5.3   TAILORING OF PRINCE2

> 3.2
> Tailoring of
> PRINCE2™

PRINCE2™ has been tailored to align to other organisational processes and is the adopted standard for all projects within the organisation.

5.3.1 P2MM content

Purpose

The purpose of Tailoring of PRINCE2 is to align the project management method to the other business processes that govern and support the project, and to develop and maintain a set of project management process assets that can be used by all projects within the organisation to improve project performance.

Key Practices

PRINCE2 is tailored to meet the specific needs of the organisation in terms of its policies, business goals, strategies and priorities.

Senior management within the organisation approves the tailoring of the PRINCE2 method.

This tailoring is documented and includes the following:

- Description of project roles
- Planning standards
- Guidance on the use of project management tools
- A library of standard Management Product Descriptions, derived from the PRINCE2 Product Outlines in Appendix A of the PRINCE2 manual.

Senior management, in a Project Board role, adopts PRINCE2 and ensures that the Project Manager follows the method.

Lessons learned on individual projects are used to identify areas where further tailoring would improve the use of PRINCE2.

Project Boards may adapt the use of PRINCE2 to meet individual project needs, based on documented guidance.

Figure 5.2 Implementation structure

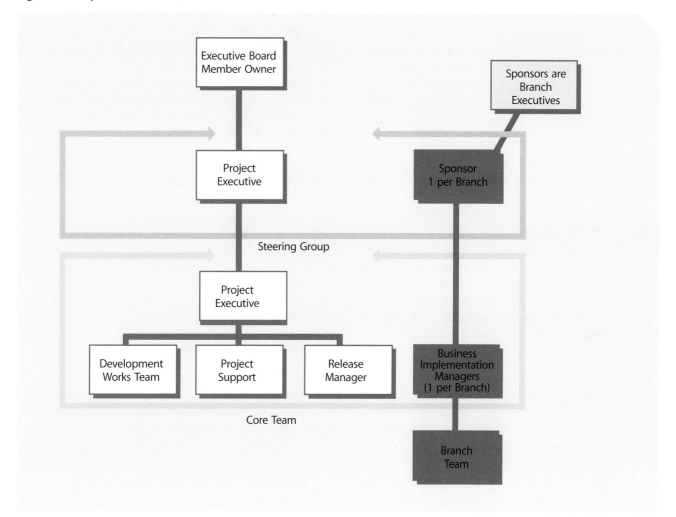

5.3.2 Guidance

What does this KPA mean?

The organisation defines how PRINCE2 will be applied and in particular how it integrates with other company processes and policies (for example, Project Approval in PRINCE2 Process DP2 should link to company rules on approving budgets or procurement. Appointing people to project management roles in PRINCE2 Process SU3 should link to the company's HR or resource management processes).

The organisation has tailored the product outlines from the PRINCE2 manual and produced associated templates that meet the needs of the organisation.

Why is this KPA necessary?

PRINCE2's strength and weakness is its flexibility. Its strength is that it can be applied to any type of project – a factor that has undoubtedly resulted in it being the most widely used method worldwide. Its weakness becomes apparent when you send 10 Project Managers on a PRINCE2 course and they produce 10 very different PIDs when they initiate their next project. This is because there are no templates in PRINCE2.

The PRINCE2 manual describes the management products that a well-managed project requires. Like the specialist products on the Product Breakdown Structure (PBS), management products are in a hierarchy. An organisation may produce a template for all of its management products at the lowest level of the management part of the PBS or manage a reduced set of collective products further up the hierarchy (e.g. a PID that has the Project Plan, Project Quality Plan, Communications Plan and Configuration Management Plan embedded within it rather than referenced).

Project documents should be specific to the needs of the project, but they also need to have a degree of consistency within the organisation if efficiencies are to be gained. For example, you have just been asked to take over a project because the existing Project Manager is about to go on maternity leave for nine months. With a consistent application of PRINCE2 you will know where to look for the project documents in order to gain a good understanding of the status of the project. The Product Checklist uses the company's standard coding so the status of the deliverables is clear (e.g. not started, in development, complete) and the Quality Log uses the company's standard annotation for the types of quality checks that are planned. The Stage Plan describes who will be undertaking those quality checks, and when.

Take another example of a Senior Manager who has 10 projects within her department. All of the Project Managers use their own flavour of PRINCE2. Each month the Senior Manager receives 10 Highlight Reports showing the status of each project. Some are received at the beginning of the month, some during and some at the end of the month. The Senior Manager needs to produce a management report for the board that includes a forecast of the department's costs and planned achievements. Not only does the Senior Manager have an issue because the currency of the information is different, but the content of the Highlight Reports is different too – some show the cumulative cost of the project, some show just the monthly expenditure, some show the external spend only, not the internal resource cost and so on.

Having a defined way of applying PRINCE2 as well as a defined set of templates (both of which are aligned to the organisation's needs) is an essential step in gaining a continuous improvement capability.

How can this KPA be implemented?

Tactics may include:

- Defining a project scorecard to assess the degree of project management overhead to apply, for example:
  - Light – a few templates, single-stage project, part-time Project Manager, small Project Board
  - Medium – most templates, perhaps multi-stage projects, part-time Project Manager, full Project Board
  - Full – nearly all templates, multi-stage projects, full-time Project Manager, Team Managers, full Project Board

- Using a project scorecard to trap those undertakings that are large tasks rather than a small project – such undertakings may benefit from using only Product Descriptions, a Work Package and some logs. Over-applying project management processes is a quick way to lose buy-in to PRINCE2

- Avoiding the temptation to rewrite the PRINCE2 manual. State your policies and standards and refer to the manual for the process content
- Finding out what processes and templates are already in use before designing the corporate set. They will be much more readily adopted if they are seen to be the best practices from across the organisation
- Making some templates mandatory for all projects in the organisation. This could be required for two reasons:
  - To enable the rollup of data into corporate reports: for example, data from every Highlight Report can be aggregated to produce a corporate status dashboard
  - A standard format helps speed-reading and understanding: for example, by presenting the Business Case in the same format and style every time, readers will know what information it contains and where to find it
- Designating some documents as mandatory at specific senior management review points. For example, when the decision is made to invest in a project, the mandatory documents could be the Business Case, PID and Risk Log. Over time, Senior Managers will become familiar with the style and content, and will increasingly demand an improvement in the quality of submitted materials. Be aware that it is the quality of the content not the quality of the template that is important. Good-looking documents may not mean they are good documents
- Embedding the project management process and templates within an enterprise tool (the process is workflow based and will become intuitive)
- Aligning the Project Initiation, Stage and Closure approvals around existing business approval rules. A gateway process will help. Where possible produce

company-specific checklists for each gateway (e.g. HR checks, facilities checks, IT support checks, and marketing checks)

- Piloting the processes and templates before launching them across the whole organisation
- Ensuring that feedback mechanisms are in place (KPA 3.5) and that additional resources are in place to review such feedback and release improved versions of processes and templates quickly in the first few months of operation (KPA 3.1). There is no better way to stifle feedback than by not acting on it quickly. Improving processes and templates will encourage more feedback. Field-based feedback is more valuable than untested ideas from people not using the processes on a day-to-day basis (e.g. the head office or the PMO).

5.3.3 Examples

London Borough of Waltham Forest

On joining Waltham Forest in 2005, Max Carter, the new e-Transformations Unit Manager was tasked with establishing a Project and Programme Management Centre of Excellence (PPM CoE). The prime purpose of the PPM CoE was to facilitate sustained improvement in the capacity and capability of the organisation to effectively govern and manage strategic projects and programmes.

One of the first responsibilities was to develop a consistent approach to project management and specifically PRINCE2. A tailored version of PRINCE2 was developed called the Waltham Forest Project Lifecycle, this included a project-sizing tool to help managers establish the size of a project based on a number of criteria (duration, effort, impact, priority, risk and cost).

Figure 5.3 Waltham Forest Project Lifecycle

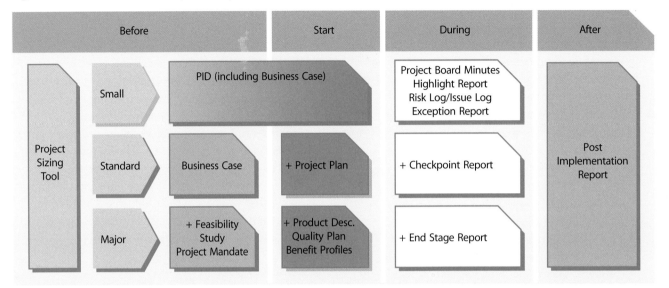

Once a project is classified as small, standard or major, the Waltham Forest Project Lifecycle then specifies the required level of documentation needed during the four key stages; before, at the start, during and after project closure (see Figure 5.3).

A conscious decision was made to deliver the Waltham Forest Project Lifecycle as a set of related intranet pages rather than a traditional project management manual, supplementing this with related bite-size guidance on particular subjects, for example, project and programme reporting.

In addition, a key aspect of the tailoring process has been to develop appropriate training internally, explaining how PRINCE2 (and the Waltham Forest PPM tool) is to be implemented across the organisation. This has been further supplemented by the introduction of a bi-monthly PPM Forum for those involved in projects across the organisation.

It was also important to ensure that the implementation of the Waltham Forest Project Lifecycle was tailored to reflect the project management maturity of the organisation. Therefore, an incremental approach was employed, initially focussing on ICT and e-Government-related projects and starting with a 'lighter touch' for other Council projects and programmes. Now that the training programme has been running for six months and awareness levels are increasing, the PPM CoE is mentoring those involved with strategic Council programmes to help further strengthen project management practices throughout the Council.

Consultancy firm

Table 5.1 shows an extract from an ISO 9001 certified QMS demonstrating how PRINCE2 management products are scaled for customer assignments.

Table 5.1 Scaling PRINCE2 by management product

Management product	Light Full	Medium	Full
Business Case	M	M	M
Checkpoint Report	O	O	M
Communications Plan	M1	M1	M1
Configuration Management Plan	O	M1	M
End Project Report	M	M	M
End Stage Report	–	O	M
Exception Report	M2	M2	M2
Highlight Report	M	M	M
Lessons Learned Report	M5	M5	M5
PID	M	M	M
Product Checklist	O	O	M
Product Description	M1	M	M
Project Brief	O1	M	M
Project Issue	M3	M3	M3
Project Mandate	O1	O	O
Project Plan	M1	M1	M
Project Quality Plan	M1	M1	M
Quality Log	O	O	M
Risk and Issue Logs	M	M	M
Stage Plan	–	M4	M
Work Package	–	O2	M

Notes

O = Optional

O1 = If the Mandate is omitted, then the Project Brief is mandatory

O2 = Optional unless external contractors are being used, then it is mandatory

M = Mandatory

M1 = Mandatory (but included as part of the PID)

M2 = Mandatory if an exception occurs

M3 = Mandatory only for issues that put the project into exception

M4 = Mandatory for multi-stage projects

M5 = Mandatory (but part of End Project Report if desired)

5.4   TRAINING IN PRINCE2

> 3.3
> Training in
> PRINCE2™

PRINCE2™ has been tailored to align to other organisational processes and is the adopted standard for all projects within the organisation.

5.4.1   P2MM content

Purpose

The purpose of Training in PRINCE2 is to develop the skills and knowledge of all members of the Project Management Team so that they can perform their roles effectively and efficiently.

Key Practices

Training needs are identified and documented for each of the Project Management Team roles:

- Project Board members (including any project assurance roles) are trained to understand their roles and responsibilities and to perform the Directing a Project process
- Project Managers are trained to Practitioner Level
- Team Managers and Project Support staff are trained to Foundation Level.

Appropriate training in the use of PRINCE2 is provided to everyone undertaking a Project Management Team role, and this is provided in a timely fashion.

Where appropriate, skills and competencies are assessed at the end of each PRINCE2 training event.

The training covers general principles of PRINCE2 and how the method has been tailored for use within the organisation.

The overall effectiveness of the PRINCE2 training is measured on an ongoing basis.

Training is also provided to help Project Managers tailor PRINCE2 for individual projects.

5.4.2 Guidance

What does this KPA mean?

Training (some of) your Project Managers in PRINCE2 is not sufficient. Their needs to be an organisation-wide approach – everyone involved in projects should have a defined level of training available to them. For some people this will be systematically applied because of their role in the organisation. For others, the training requirement might be triggered by a temporary appointment to a project role. At least one element of the training should be specific to the way in which the organisation has implemented PRINCE2.

Why is this KPA necessary?

As mentioned for KPA 2.6 (Organisation), projects are a people thing. You can't have a project if you don't have any people involved. No amount of good planning or control will help if the people involved do not know what's expected of them or don't have the competencies required to be able to meet their project duties.

A training and development strategy is required to:

- Ensure the right amount of training is provided according to the different roles
- Achieve a common understanding of PRINCE2 across your organisation when first implementing it
- Accommodate people who are changing role (and potentially are faced with project duties that are new to them) after the implementation
- Accommodate people joining the organisation after the implementation
- Identify further areas of training need (e.g. soft skills).

Inappropriate training is a massive drain on an organisation. For example, in the UK when the Audit Commission conducted the first round of Comprehensive Performance Assessments (CPA) of Local Authorities, most of the reports recommended improving project management capability. A rush of PRINCE2 training ensued and Service Heads could sometimes be found attending Foundation training (a three-day programme) or Practitioner training (five days). 'I'm supposed to manage some Project Managers. How can I tell them what to do if they know more about managing projects than I do?' was often the reason given. Denying an organisation a Senior Manager unnecessarily for three or five days is a terrible waste, especially when one or two days of focused training on the directing and decision-making duties of Project Board members would yield better results.

In the private sector on the other hand, trying to get two hours of a Senior Manager's time can prove difficult. It is not surprising in such cases to see projects struggle when Project Board members are not familiar with the controls available to them. Examples of zero tolerance, project assurance being delegated to Project Managers and 'try harder' responses to Exception Reports are unfortunately common observations when projects are governed in ignorance.

How can this KPA be implemented?

Tactics may include:

- An initial skills assessment to find out how many of the Project Managers already have PRINCE2 training, qualifications, or experience
- Deciding what level of training is required (is certification important?)
- Applying a top-down approach so that Senior Managers support the training rollout to their staff
- Piloting training events with 'friendly' departments
- Incorporating PRINCE2 briefings into induction training
- Further competency assessments to identify advanced or specialist training beyond the initial rollout
- Linking training courses with personal development plans and performance objectives (e.g. if you attend these courses then these are the results we expect to see). The expected performance improvements should be reviewed about three to six months after the training
- Providing Project Managers with training materials that they can use in start-up or initiation workshops to brief Project Board members or project team members new to PRINCE2. They should come away from the workshops with sufficient understanding to be able to contribute to the project and know what is expected of them

- Establishing an in-house training capability within your project management office or centre of excellence.

5.4.3 Examples

A metropolitan borough council

When a large metropolitan borough council decided to implement PRINCE2, it conducted a survey of the organisation to understand its project management landscape.

The council discovered that it had more than 400 people managing projects, but 380 of them also had a 'day job' and only 85 had had any formal training in project management. The council also identified that it had a diverse portfolio of projects ranging from a small team with a purchase budget of less than £1000 for a project lasting only a few weeks at one end of the scale, to a project involving a large multi-organisational team, with a budget in excess of £300 million and lasting six years at the other end. There wasn't a typical project. Consequently, the training needs were not uniform.

The council implemented a top-down approach starting with Project Board training for the Leadership Forum, which included more than 40 Senior Managers who sponsored projects or who had Project Managers working for them. PRINCE2 overviews combined with an introduction to project management were provided for people who managed projects (which covered most of the 400 staff). Armed with a better understanding of projects and project management, the Senior Managers then identified who within their teams should receive more advanced training, including the PRINCE2 Practitioner training.

Manchester City Council

Manchester City Council started its PRINCE2 implementation in 2002. The training strategy initially comprised:

- Two-day courses for Project Managers and half-day briefing sessions for board members (to date nearly 1000 staff have been trained)
- Follow-on Foundation and Practitioner courses for selected Project Managers (more than 50 trained to date).

The top-down approach was considered a key factor in the success of the 'Manchester Method', which went on to win the National Training Awards 2005 and was a finalist in the APM awards in 2005.

However, as the council rolled out updates to the method and raised the level of compliance expected, it discovered that it needed further training modules:

- Consistency on progress reporting – what does Red, Amber, Green mean?
- Project accounting (expenditure tracking).

The next phase (the fourth) of the implementation journey is to establish a centre of excellence capable of managing major projects and providing in-house consultancy to other services within the council. As part of this phase the council has initiated risk management training for their internal consultants (to facilitate risk workshops).

5.5 INTEGRATED MANAGEMENT

3.4 Integrated Management

PRINCE2™ has been tailored to align to other organisational processes and is the adopted standard for all projects within the organisation.

5.5.1 P2MM content

Purpose

The purpose of Integrated Management is to ensure that all project activities form a coherent set based on the PRINCE2 method. It necessitates the development of a Project Initiation Document that takes into account the project's size, schedule and staffing. The emphasis is on anticipating problems and minimising their effects.

Key Practices

There is an organisational policy requiring all projects to use PRINCE2. In particular:

- Every project has an Initiation Stage
- During this stage a PID is produced that identifies the customer's quality expectations and acceptance criteria
- Tolerances are agreed by all members of the Project Management Team
- Projects are broken down into subsequent stages that are planned, monitored and controlled in accordance with PRINCE2
- Formal reviews are undertaken at the end of each stage
- Projects are closed in an orderly fashion as prescribed by PRINCE2.

Any variations from PRINCE2 are documented and approved.

Adequate resources are provided to enable projects to be managed in accordance with PRINCE2.

5.5.2 Guidance

What does this KPA mean?

A policy should be defined, complementing KPA 3.2 'Tailoring of PRINCE2', to ensure that certain minimum standards are met by all projects using the tailored version of PRINCE2. For example, every project should have an initiation stage, a PID, defined and agreed tolerances, Management Stages with End Stage Reviews, and a controlled close.

To ensure a common understanding of the project management approach applied on any given project there should be a policy in force to ensure that any variations from PRINCE2 and the tailored version are documented.

Why is this KPA necessary?

As mentioned in section 5.3.2, if you send 10 Project Managers on a PRINCE2 course they will produce 10 very different PIDs when they initiate their next project. This is because there are very few mandatory elements to PRINCE2.

As an extreme example, you could argue that if you have at least two stages, the first of which is an initiation stage, and you have a project organisation structure that separates out the responsibilities for directing a project and managing a project then you have a PRINCE2 project. There is more to it than that however.

P2MM defines the minimum standards to be adopted by an organisation for it to be considered mature in the application of PRINCE2:

- The initiation activities (as defined by PRINCE2's IP processes), including a formal stop/go review requiring the project to justify its continuation
- The presence of a PID, which includes:
  - Agreement of the customer's quality expectations
  - Agreement of project tolerances

- Management Stages and End Stage Reviews
- Closure activities (as defined by PRINCE2's CP processes), culminating in a formal acceptance that the project is closed
- The approval and recording of any variance to PRINCE2.

However, one size does not fit all. Each organisation needs to define and implement its own policies to clarify the minimum requirements for the application of PRINCE2 according to the different types of project it may have.

How can this KPA be implemented?

Tactics may include:

- A project scorecard or sizing tool to ascertain the degree of PRINCE2 application warranted by the project
- A definition of minimum requirements by project type (simple, medium, complex?)
  - A different PID template (or set of templates) for each project type
  - Reporting requirements for each project type
  - Approval requirements for each project type
  - Ownership requirements for each project type (e.g. who should be on the board)
- Establishing Project Approval and Initiation Approval gates to include the decision on the minimum standards required of the project
- PID templates including a section in which to document any variations
- Establishing a project closure gate, ensuring that the decision to accept closure is recorded.

5.5.3 Examples

Manchester City Council

When Manchester City Council implemented PRINCE2, the 'Manchester Method' was rolled out in a phased approach over a four-year period:

- Phase 1 – Develop a standardised framework and train people in the use of the framework
- Phase 2 – Introduction (and administration) of a gateway process for project scrutiny and approval
- Phase 3 – To automate the project management process with collaboration software
- Phase 4 – To create a centre of excellence for project delivery.

Phase 1 provided the council with a definition of the degree to which PRINCE2 should be applied for each type of project. But the introduction of the gateway process in Phase 2 ensured that it was rigorously applied. Furthermore, the introduction of the collaboration tool meant that the minimum controls were now enforced through the tools: it is not possible to initiate a project without meeting the controls expected of each project type.

The Manchester City Council gateway process comprises the following:

0 Idea (Mandate)

1 Strategic fit (Gateway Review Group)

2 Corporate fit (Strategic Management Team)

3 Bid appraisal (Gateway Review Group)

4 Budget approval (Executive and Council)

5 Capital spend approval (Capital Team and Executive Member Finance)

6 Project completion (practical completion)

7 Project closure (financial completion)

8 Benefits realisation (assessment of accrued benefits, unexpected benefits and those forecase/pending).

The timing of Gateway 8 is decided at the project closure review (Gateway 7), as it will vary depending on the project context. For example, some regeneration projects can take years before the benefits can be fully assessed. Gateway 8 also ensures that the difference between actual benefits and forecast benefits are fed back into developing Business Cases (Gateway 3) for new projects. The forecasting of benefits based on previous performance helps with funding and grant applications.

5.6 QUALITY ASSURANCE

> 3.5
> Quality
> Assurance

PRINCE2™ has been tailored to align to other organisational processes and is the adopted standard for all projects within the organisation.

5.6.1 P2MM content

Purpose

The purpose of Quality Assurance is to provide an organisational assurance that the project has suitable quality plans and measures, in line with the tailored PRINCE2 method, to ensure that the project processes are suitably controlled and are likely to result in products that meet explicit quality criteria as defined by Product Descriptions.

Key Practices

The Quality Assurance Group monitors the application of PRINCE2 across all projects within the organisation.

The Quality Assurance Group is independent of the organisation's project and operational activities.

The Quality Assurance Group reviews Project Quality Plans and makes recommendations to improve the plans and, consequently, the likelihood of quality deliverables.

Quality Assurance reviews assess whether:

- The appropriate skills and competencies are in place
- Risks are being managed effectively
- Feasible and economic contingency measures are in place.

Peer reviews are conducted to encourage shared learning across projects. Peer reviews:

- Are led by trained review leaders
- Focus on the project deliverables
- Are adequately resourced.

5.6.2 Guidance

What does this KPA mean?

The pioneers of maturity modelling Watts S. Humphrey and Phil Crosby demonstrated, 'The quality of a [software] application is directly related to the quality of the process used to develop it'. The correlation between process quality and output quality holds true for all processes. Therefore if we can monitor the quality of an organisation's project management process we can predict the quality of the project's outputs. This KPA concerns the establishment of such a monitoring capability.

Why is this KPA necessary?

Investing in the adoption of PRINCE2 without subsequently monitoring the quality of its application is analogous to buying a Ferrari and leaving it in a neighbour's garage. No real value will be gained from having it. The handbook, templates and tools may just become pretty 'shelf-ware' and, unlike the Ferrari, they will depreciate in value over time.

Regular assessment of the effectiveness of your project management process will provide you with a continuous improvement capability. The evidence gathered and the conclusions drawn can be used to recommend improvements (based on field use) to your PRINCE2 implementation. Committing to implementing the improvements (KPA 3.1) will demonstrate the importance that the organisation places on them, which will in turn increase their level of adoption.

Changes to your PRINCE2 implementation should be based on metrics and user feedback. Use of a non-empirical approach may or may not improve the quality of your project's outputs – it may be a matter of luck.

Establishing a systematic way of assessing how well projects are applying your tailored version of PRINCE2 will reduce the amount of time that Project Board members need to spend to gain the same level of confidence.

How can this KPA be implemented?

Tactics may include:

- Establishing a Quality Assurance group (this might be part of an existing QA function or part of a newly formed project management office or centre of excellence (KPA 3.1). The project management office or centre of excellence may be run by staff who are seconded on a rotating basis as part of their development plans (KPA 3.3)
- Setting up an audit programme to inspect a number of sample projects each quarter
  - Audit checklists based on Appendix D of the PRINCE2 manual
  - Audit checklists based on the Level 2 checklists within this guide (to give a continuous assessment capability
- Modifying the Project Register (KPA 1.1) to include evidence of key products (such as Business Case, PID, Project Quality Plan, logs, the number of days since the last Project Board review, etc.)

- Mandating that PIDs and other plans are subject to a peer review prior to being submitted for sign-off. Peer reviews may be provided by other Project Managers within the same department, other departments or even from a centre of excellence/project management office
- Identifying people within your organisation able to chair Quality Reviews (as defined in the PRINCE2 manual) and allowing them time to prepare such reviews
- Defining standards for Quality Reviews of technical products (e.g. the use of external/third-party technical assurance expertise if the customer organisation is dependent on the supplier expertise)
- Setting up monthly, quarterly or annual conferences or workshops for the project management community to share best practices.

5.6.3 Examples

Sun Microsystems Inc.

Sun implemented PRINCE2 across its UK operations in 1998 and established an audit programme to measure its adoption and to gather feedback from the project management and business management community. Sun established an audit regime whereby the sample of projects audited was sufficient to cover all of the Project Managers every 18 months (about 15 projects were audited per quarter). The results of the audits were presented each quarter to a Quality Assurance group, which reviewed the activities against the following categories:

- Project-specific corrective action required
- Project management process/tool corrective action required
- Skills deficiency – training and development action required

- Business issue – outside the scope of project management, therefore referred to senior management.

In the four years that the UK audit programme operated in this way the project management handbook and associated processes moved from version 1.0, 1.1, 1.2, 1.3, 2.0 to 3.0. In each instance the handbook contained fewer pages than the previous version and was better targeted at the types of projects managed by the organisation. The value of the continuous improvement process was evident in that the UK project management standards – including the audit programme – were adopted by Sun as a global standard.

The audit programme has since been updated and incorporates P2MM and P1M3 indicators so that Sun's maturity can be monitored alongside compliance with its own project management standard.

P2MM assessment

6

6 P2MM assessment

6.1 OVERVIEW

There are a number of ways an organisation can assess its maturity in PRINCE2. These can be categorised as accreditation assessments and non-accreditation assessments.

Accreditation assessments result in the award of a certificate reflecting the level of maturity attained. Section 6.3.1 looks at the reasons why an organisation may seek independent verification of their maturity in PRINCE2. These assessments are typically employed at the end of the implementation initiative to embed PRINCE2 in an organisation.

Non-accreditation assessments are conducted internally or externally, usually for the purpose of measurement and diagnosis. They are used to determine current capability in order to identify where further improvements can be made.

6.2 NON-ACCREDITATION ASSESSMENT

6.2.1 Reasons for non-accreditation assessments

Gaining an understanding of your maturity against P2MM can be used to:

- Identify root causes of persistent project performance issues
- Assess baseline capability in order to formulate an improvement plan (see section 2.1.1)
- Measure progress against an improvement plan (see section 2.1.4)
- Assess readiness for an accreditation assessment (see section 6.3)
- Compare one business unit with another.

Such assessments can be conducted by Registered Consultants (see section 6.4) or by internal consultants using the method below and the checklists in Appendix A. In either case it is recommended that these assessments are considered part of an improvement project to ensure that the organisation gains benefit from them (see section 2.2). The production of a report alone will not provide tangible benefits. Tangible benefits will only come from acting on the findings of the assessment. Formal verification of P2MM maturity can be achieved only as part of an accreditation assessment (see section 6.3).

6.2.2 Approach

Snapshot assessment

The checklists in Appendix A can be used to gain a snapshot of your organisation's capability. You will need to assess a sample of projects to determine the level of adoption of PRINCE2 (Level 2 KPAs) and to assess organisational activities (Level 1 and Level 3 KPAs) to drive and support its adoption.

Continuous assessment

To gain an assessment of progress being made you can either re-run the snapshot assessment periodically or establish mechanisms to assess capability as part of an audit programme (part of KPA 3.5 – see section 5.6). Implementing continuous assessment can be achieved by incorporating the maturity indicators in Appendix A into the metrics you collect for each project (e.g. include the Level 2 maturity indicators in the Project Quality Plan template, review them as part of the End Stage Assessments and End Project Assessment, use them as the basis for Quality Assurance assessments).

The advantage of a continuous assessment process is that it encourages good practices to be continuously applied, not just in the lead-up to an annual or quarterly assessment. Additionally, if integrated (and automated) within a wider regime of collecting metrics for your organisation, the cost of the assessment will reduce.

Trend analysis

Regardless whether you choose a continuous or a snapshot approach to assessments, you should track your direction of travel as well as your current position. Performance can go down as well as up! It may be that there have been organisational changes, the implementation of a new tool, changes to the reward and bonus system, or other internal or external changes that can have an impact on your project management capability. Such changes may require your project management policies, processes and templates to be reviewed, amended and re-deployed to maintain your level of maturity.

Additionally, comparing the individual maturity of the autonomous business units (departments, divisions, offices, etc.) across your organisation may help to identify good practices that can be shared or may be used to identify those parts of your organisation that need greater management focus (remember that maturity models are a predictor of performance).

6.2.3 Method for snapshot assessment

Scope

First, define the parts of your organisation that are subject to assessment and the types of projects you will assess. The terms of reference for the assessment need to be agreed so that the people conducting the assessment (whether external or internal) have sufficient authority and access to project personnel and data. The timescale for the assessment should also be agreed. If the snapshot

assessment is part of a periodic assessment you may wish to rotate the area of focus for each assessment (e.g. conducting a quick review of all KPAs, but a detailed assessment of one or two specific KPAs each time).

Plan

The assessment should include:

- A review of relevant policies, processes and supporting tools
- Interviews with a sample group of Project Managers, Project Executives and project management office staff
- A review of project documentation (for the sample projects).

The size and breakdown of the sample will determine the number and type of people you will need to interview. Base your sample on the recommendations for an accreditation assessment (see section 6.3.3). Experience shows that you should allow four hours to interview the Head of Projects (or equivalent), and two hours to interview Project Managers and Project Executives.

Inspect

Use the appropriate checklists in Appendix A:

- Level 2 KPA checklists for each project in the sample
- Level 3 KPA checklists for your project management office (or equivalent).

Remember that Level 2 maturity is achieved when most of your projects are using PRINCE2 (even if inconsistently) and Level 3 maturity is achieved when all of your projects are applying your adapted version of PRINCE2. Ensure that mechanisms are in place to provide ownership, alignment to your organisational processes and structures and continuous improvement.

As an assessor look for:

- Documents with suspicious dates (e.g. several documents produced the day before an assessment)

- Documents with generic content (has content been cut and paste from the last project or has the same template been used with a name change?)
- Documents still at version 1.0 (this might be ok, but experience suggests that further questions should be asked)
- Approvals being granted in arrears (e.g. projects starting prior to agreement)

- People who are unaware that they have been assigned to a project (or a particular role on the project)
- People who are consistently unavailable for interview
- Actions allocated to just a few people.

With this in mind, the information contained in Table 6.1 can be a helpful aid when assessing indicators of conformance.

Table 6.1 Examples of evidence

Item	Non-compliance	Partial compliance	Full compliance
Documents	No document exists	Document exists but may not be under formal control (perhaps still at draft revision)	A standard document is used, is formally controlled and adds value to the project
	Document exists but with no evidence it was issued	Document exists but is out of date (e.g. PID was not updated after End Stage Review)	An equivalent but non-standard document is used (and its use is recorded in the PID and agreed by the Project Board)
	Document exists but is purely a cut and paste from the template and is not specific to the project	An equivalent but non-standard document is used	
Reviews	No evidence that the review took place	The review took place but was not formally recorded	The review took place, is formally recorded (e.g. there is evidence of minutes, end reports or updated documents) and actions have been acted on (as recorded in the logs)
Logs	Logs do not exist	Logs exist but are not up-to-date (e.g. risks appear in the Highlight Reports, but not in the Risk Log)	Logs exist and accurately reflect the status of the project
	Logs exist but have not been updated since the start of the project		
Organisation	People are assigned to roles in name only	People are assigned to roles but may not have the authority, capability or capacity to discharge their responsibilities	People are assigned to roles and have the authority, capability or capacity to discharge their responsibilities
			People understand what's expected of them and what to expect of others (and this matches the definitions in the PID)

Analyse

When aggregating the project assessments (Level 2 KPAs), they should be reviewed against the characteristics of Level 2 maturity (i.e. are they repeatable?). Bear in mind that there are shades of grey in terms of how many projects constitute 'most' for example. Applying the scoring mechanism used for the accreditation assessment (see section 6.3.3) will help prepare the way for a formal assessment if one is planned for later.

The organisational assessments (Level 3 KPAs) are defined by the characteristics of Level 3 maturity (i.e. are they consistent?) and therefore scoring is more black and white (e.g. either you have a Project Management Handbook or not; it has been reviewed and updated in the last year or not).

6.3 ACCREDITATION ASSESSMENT

6.3.1 Reasons

The first maturity model was developed as a means for the US Government to make better procurement decisions by comparing contractors' capabilities. P2MM can be used in the same way. If you tender for government business, procurement professionals give more credence to an independently awarded certificate than a company's own claims of capability. Procurement professionals may give more weight to an organisational certificate than they do an individual's certificate. Currently organisations submit PRINCE2 Practitioner certificates with their proposal as an indicator of project management capability. With more than 250,000 PRINCE2 Practitioners worldwide, however, it is difficult for buyers to differentiate between them.

Just like gaining ISO 9001 or IIP accreditation, there are benefits for customer organisations gaining accreditation in PRINCE2 maturity too, as it:

- Demonstrates commitment to PRINCE2 and its importance within the organisation

- Provides evidence for regulators
- Helps recruitment by attracting good people (acting as a differentiator)
- Improves morale through increased corporate pride.

6.3.2 Assessment approach

An accreditation assessment should be carried out only after an organisation has implemented PRINCE2. It verifies how well the method has been implemented. An organisation wishing to gauge current capability in order to plan improvements in its application of PRINCE2 should consider a self-assessment or baseline assessment first (see sections 2.1.1 and 6.2).

The main consideration for an accreditation assessment is its scope. Should/could the assessment cover your whole organisation or will it be better by department, branch, division, business unit, etc. For example:

- Vodafone gained P2MM Level 3 accreditation for a particular area of Vodafone – the Telecom Systems Department (TS) of Vodafone UK Technology. TS had more than 130 concurrent projects with an annual spend of over £100 million and accordingly was responsible for how it managed its projects[7].
- The Pension Protection Fund[8] was a newly formed organisation with a single project management office for all of the projects within the organisation. It gained P3M3 and P2MM Level 3 for the entire organisation.

As you can see, the level of autonomy that each part of your organisation has will affect your approach to assessment. It is typical for multinationals to set a global standard for project management. This standard is likely to be set by and under the control of a project management office, which will then request that each region, country or business unit implements those standards. The central project management office may provide advice on implementation, but will leave the finer detail to the business units. An organisation with 12 autonomous business units is highly likely to see a different level of maturity in each. Conducting a single assessment for the global organisation will mean that the results will be averaged and will therefore be somewhat meaningless. In such a case it would be far more effective to assess the level of maturity of each autonomous business unit. The business unit dashboard will show the status of each KPA (e.g. 11 of the 16 KPAs are fully compliant, four are partially compliant and one is non-compliant), but the global dashboard will show the maturity level of each business unit (e.g. nine of the 12 business units are at Level 3).

When conducting assessments across a large organisation, identify which of the organisational questions need to be asked only at the corporate level and which should be directed to each of the autonomous business units. For example, if there is a single corporate standard for project management, the assessors need to review this only once. The project-level questions should be asked of all business units. (See section 6.3.3 for an explanation of the organisational and project-level questions.)

6.3.3 Assessment method

The OGC's accreditation partner the APM Group has used P2MM to establish an accreditation process for gauging the maturity level of an organisation's implementation and application of PRINCE2.

To gain P2MM accreditation an organisation needs to engage the services of an Accredited Consulting Organisation (ACO) to undertake the assessment. The assessment must be led by qualified consultants (Registered Consultants) who have been assessed for their knowledge, experience and expertise and who have been trained to carry out P2MM assessment. The assessment must also be carried out in accordance with the APM Group's accreditation process, which requires Registered Consultants to apply a consistent approach to interviews and evidence assessments. The process itself is subject to accreditation, having been assessed by the United Kingdom Accreditation Service (UKAS).

At or before the start-up of the assignment, the Registered Consultant is required to obtain:

- A definitive list of projects indicating the scale of each project. Based on this list the Registered Consultant will select, in conjunction with the client, a definitive list of people to be interviewed
- A set of the organisation's processes and procedures covering the management of its projects.

During the assessment the consultants follow a process of evidence gathering and structured interviews, as defined in the APM Group's Quality Manual, to determine whether the organisation exhibits the practices expected of the KPAs in P2MM.

The accreditation process takes the form of a Stage 1 and Stage 2 assessment. The Stage 1 assessment identifies the organisation's approximate level of maturity in project management. A Stage 1 questionnaire is administered by the Registered Consultant and requires the most senior person with project responsibility to provide honest answers. The Stage 1 questionnaire isolates the highest level of maturity that the organisation is likely to achieve in the Stage 2 assessment.

If an organisation is unlikely to achieve Level 2 maturity in the Stage 2 assessment, it means that project management is not a yet core capability within the organisation. Instead of continuing with the accreditation assessment, it is recommended that a project is initiated to implement project management (see Chapter 2).

Figure 6.1 Accreditation process

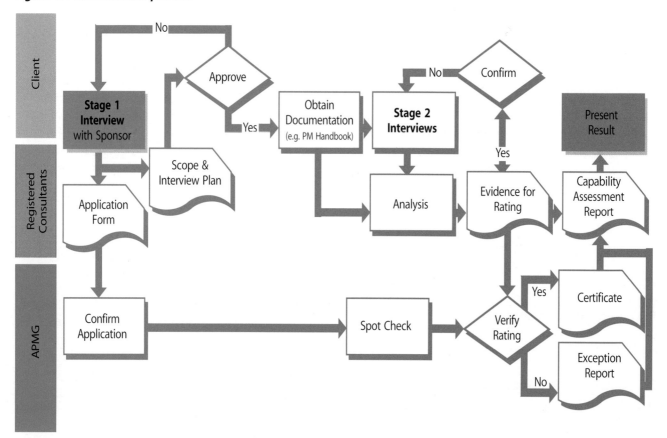

The number of people interviewed at Stage 2 is dependent on the size of the organisation and the average number of concurrent projects under way. Table 6.2 specifies the minimum number of interviews required for an accreditation assessment based on the number of ongoing projects for each participant.

Table 6.2 Minimum number of interviews required for each role

Interviewees	Number of concurrent projects			
	< 5	6 to 20	21 to 50	> 50
Head of Projects	1	1	1	1
Head of Projects Office	1	1	1	1
Project Executives	1	2	2	2
Project Managers	2	4	6	8

The Registered Consultants are not expecting to see people with job titles matching those in Table 6.2 exactly, but those people with corresponding responsibilities.

The Stage 2 interviews are subject to a spot-check by the APM Group lead assessor who will wish to witness a day of interviewing by the Registered Consultant during the assignment. If during the Stage 2 interviews there are only a few non-conformities preventing the next level of maturity certification, the Registered Consultant may suggest implementing a remedial plan and follow-up verification prior to submitting the results to the APM Group.

The assessment is based on the answers to up to 30 questions, some of which relate to the organisation as a whole and others of which are project specific. The type of questions asked will depend on the type of role performed by the interviewee (see Table 6.3).

Table 6.3 Question sets according to role

	Interview question sets	
	Set 1 – Organisational	Set 2 – Projects
Head of Projects	Yes	Yes
Head of Projects Office	Yes	
Project Executives	Subset	Subset
Project Manager		Yes

The Registered Consultants will aggregate the interview responses to rate the answers to the 30 questions in the following bands:

- Yes always (more than 90%)
- Yes sometimes (more than 60%)
- Not always (more than 20%)
- Never (less than 20%).

To achieve a maturity level:

- The organisation must have NO 'Never' scores at the level sought
- All answers must score at least 'Not always'
- All key questions MUST score at least 'Yes sometimes'.

The Registered Consultant's findings and recommendations are submitted to the APM Group for verification. Subject to meeting the minimum standards, the APM Group will issue a certificate for the level of maturity attained in accordance with the company's UKAS accreditation. The certificate is valid for three years and requires a minor annual external audit. After three years, the full accreditation assessment will need to be repeated.

A fee is payable by the client to the APM Group for each accreditation application. This entitles the organisation to use the certificate and relevant logos (e.g. PRINCE2) in its marketing material. The current fees can be found on the APM Group website.

6.3.4 Assessment scope

The OGC's maturity models are nested (see Figure 6.2). The APM Group assessment method can be applied to P2MM only (PRINCE2), P1M3 (+Projects), P2M3 (+Programmes) and P3M3 (+Portfolios). Maturity certificates can be awarded at different levels for each model with the proviso that you cannot have a higher P2M3 level than your P1M3 and you cannot have a higher P3M3 level than your P2M3.

6.4 FINDING AN ACCREDITED CONSULTING ORGANISATION

General

Accredited Consulting Organisations (ACOs) employ experienced consultants who have been assessed on their knowledge of PRINCE2, are recommended by the APM Group and the OGC to provide advice on PRINCE2 and are also qualified to assess organisations using the PRINCE2

Figure 6.2 Nested OGC maturity models

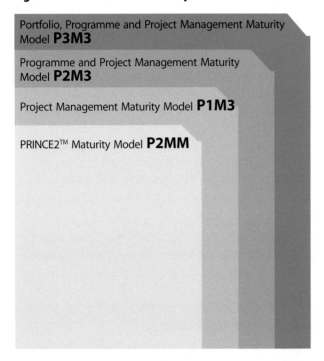

Portfolio, Programme and Project Management Maturity Model **P3M3**

Programme and Project Management Maturity Model **P2M3**

Project Management Maturity Model **P1M3**

PRINCE2™ Maturity Model **P2MM**

Maturity Model (P2MM). Such consultants are known as PRINCE2 Registered Consultants or P2RCs.

ACOs have also undergone a full assessment by the APM Group of their organisation's management systems and processes for undertaking consultancy assignments.

Eligibility of an ACO

To be eligible for certification as an ACO, an organisation must meet, and continue to meet, the following criteria:

- Have run at least one project management consultancy assignment within the 12 months prior to the date of application. For organisations that have been trading for less than two years, at least one director or senior employee must have run three or more consultancy assignments within the previous 36 months.
- At all times, undertake to have only Registered Consultants leading any PRINCE2 assignment. Non-registered consultants can assist Registered Consultants to deliver consulting assignments.
- At all times, have at least one consultant meeting the eligibility criteria for approved status as described below.

Eligibility of PRINCE2 Registered Consultants

A PRINCE2 Registered Consultant will need to:

- Have two years' experience in management consultancy services in general and two years' experience in the PRINCE2 method in particular
- Demonstrate knowledge of PRINCE2 by having a high pass mark on the PRINCE2 Practitioner exam
- Be able to provide four valid professional referees
- Be able to present full oral evidence of at least one completed management consultancy assignment
- Be able to present full oral evidence of at least one completed PRINCE2 consultancy assignment
- Be able to provide a portfolio of evidence to show that the required standards can be met
- Promote a professional image, particularly when presenting ideas and findings to a client.

ACO listing

A list of ACOs can be found on the APM Group website: www.prince2.org.uk

At the time of publication there are 16 ACOs able to conduct accreditation assessments in PRINCE2.

6.5 EXAMPLES

To guide an implementation

The following is an extract from a case study written by Kate Winter of the APM Group, August 2006[8].

The Pension Protection Fund (PPF) is a UK public corporation that pays compensation to people when their defined pension scheme collapses. The PPF became operational on 6 April 2005. After about six months it decided to set up a project management office, straddling both business and IT projects, in order to gain control of the pace of change and the rate of growth that the organisation was experiencing.

PPF wanted to implement PRINCE2 and Managing Successful Programmes (MSP) at the same time, so for help the company turned to P2MM and P3M3 as a model of what a good implementation should look like.

The company achieved Level 3 accreditation in both P2MM and P3M3 in just over six months. Gaining the accreditation gave the embryonic organisation greater confidence that it was approaching projects and programmes in the right way. With pensions very much in the public eye, gaining a Level 3 benchmark provides reassurance that the public's money is being spent wisely.

However, 'It's not the accreditation that matters, it's the journey', according to the PPF's former project management office manager Dominic Joyce shortly after receiving P2MM Level 3 accreditation.

To gain recognition

The following is an extract from a presentation given by Hans N. J. Smit, President Director, Port of Rotterdam, at the Best Practice Showcase in June 2005[9].

Rotterdam is Europe's largest logistic and industrial hub. The port is the gateway to a European market of 450 million consumers. More than 500 scheduled services link Rotterdam with over 1000 ports worldwide. Throughput in 2005 amounted to 370 million tonnes.

The port of Rotterdam is investing all the time to expand and improve its service. The most high-profile project is the pending construction of Maasvlakte 2 (MV2), a new port and industrial zone in the North Sea, providing 1000 hectares of industrial sites with direct access to deep waters.

The MV2 project is one of the largest infrastructure projects in the Netherlands. However, because of a track record of spiralling costs, negative public opinion surrounds large infrastructure projects in the Netherlands. The Dutch government therefore monitors large infrastructure projects closely. The MV2 project aimed to set a 'best practice' standard for such projects. PRINCE2 was chosen as the project management methodology to be used because of its focus on the Business Case and the separation of Directing and Managing the project. Tight timescales meant that PRINCE2 had to be adopted quickly and having done so, the MV2 project team wanted to check that it was using PRINCE2 appropriately. The team commissioned an accreditation assessment against P2MM.

The MV2 project gained Level 2 P2MM certification and an improvement plan of what was required to move to Level 3. The accreditation gave confidence to the stakeholders and the public that the project was set up and controlled effectively during initiation. The accreditation was also important to show to stakeholders, such as the Dutch government, that the project continues to be well controlled. The accreditation is also named in the decision of the Dutch Cabinet regarding the investment in the MV2 project and is seen as a very important value. The accreditation helped the project organisation to focus on what else was required to gain further value from the use of PRINCE2. Drs. R. Moret, PRINCE2 Registered Consultant, carried out the accreditation.

To revitalise an existing implementation

The following is an extract from a presentation given at the Best Practice User Group by Tony Church, Professional Services Delivery Manager of Sun Microsystems Inc., in November 2004.

Sun's professional services group exists to help clients implement and gain benefit from their IT solutions. As such most of their project work centres around the implementation of Sun hardware and software. Sun implemented PRINCE2 in its UK operations 1998 and quickly established best practices in the use of PRINCE2. In 2003/4 the UK's implementation of PRINCE2 was adopted across the corporation as part of an initiative to standardise its management systems globally for Sarbanes-Oxley compliance.

Operations in each country were required to take the global standard and 'localise' it to integrate it with local policies, structures and systems. The rollout of the new project management standard coincided with changes to the organisation and management team in the UK. Previous project management practices that had become institutionalised no longer applied to the new structures, management team and corporate method. The UK, which had been a beacon country within Sun, struggled to apply the new standards.

Sun decided to undertake an assessment against P2MM and P3M3 to ascertain the UK's strengths and weaknesses and to identify how to regain its best practice application of PRINCE2. The assessment showed that the people skills were above those required for Level 3 maturity. The systems maturity was above that required for Level 3, but the processes required some clarification. The main conclusion drawn from the assessment was a need to align the PRINCE2 Project Board roles (of Executive, User and Supplier) to senior people within the organisation whose objectives generate the type of behaviour expected of that project role. Sun has initiated an improvement plan based on the analysis, has already improved performance, and aims to undergo accreditation assessment in 2007.

7

Beyond P2MM

7 Beyond P2MM

In 2003 the OGC released its first draft of a Portfolio, Programme and Project Management Maturity Model (P3M3). The model was refined and formally published in February 2006 after incorporating the latest CMMI® practices and after consultation with interested consultants, practitioners and its accreditation partner the APM Group.

P3M3 describes the portfolio-, programme- and project-related activities within each process area that contribute to consistently achieving successful project outcomes. The levels described within P3M3 indicate how Key Process Areas can be structured hierarchically to define a progression of capability that an organisation can use to set goals and plan its improvement journey.

The 32 Key Process Areas in P3M3 (see Figure 7.1) provide a greater level of detail than in P2MM and have the following common features:

■ Functional achievement/process goals
■ Approach
■ Deployment
■ Review
■ Perception
■ Performance measures.

The distinct yet connected disciplines of portfolio, programme and project management are nested within the P3M3 model.

This means that organisations can use the model to evolve their maturity across all disciplines in an integrated approach by addressing project management, programme management and portfolio management in parallel (rather than doing projects, then programmes, then portfolio in

sequence). There is a lot of merit in this approach as the portfolio and programme KPAs will help identify the right projects, whereas the project KPAs identify how to deliver those projects successfully.

Just as PRINCE2 is a subset of the wider project management body of knowledge, so P2MM is a subset of the Portfolio, Programme and Project Management Maturity Model (P3M3). P2MM does not fully cover requirements management, stakeholder management, management of suppliers or benefits management for example.

Figure 7.2 shows the P3M3 KPAs in which an organisation can expect to demonstrate maturity if it has already achieved P2MM Level 3 accreditation.

The contribution that implementing PRINCE2 has on an organisation's wider Project and Programme Management capability is neatly illustrated in Figure 7.2. The diagram shows why PRINCE2 should not be seen as the only answer to increasing an organisation's project management capability. It does provide a great jump-start though – as evidenced by the Pension Protection Fund's jump from zero to Level 3 in six months (see section 6.5).

Achieving Level 3 compliance in P3M3 would enable organisations to meet all 11 governance principles recommended by the Association for Project Management[4].

Figure 7.1 Portfolio, Programme and Project Management Maturity Model (P3M3)

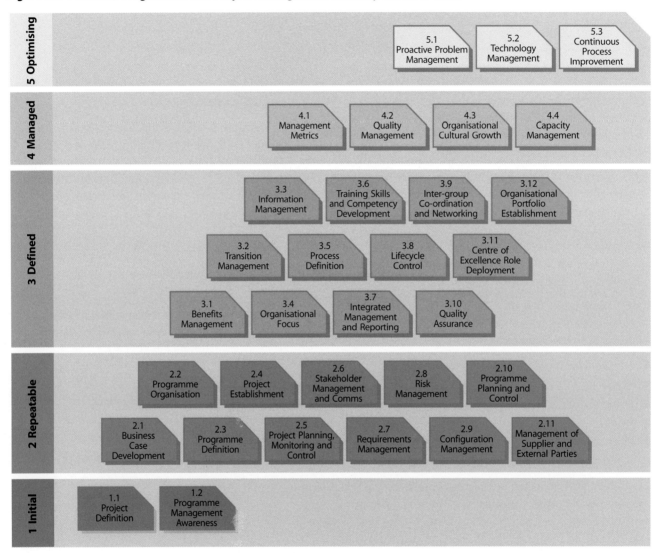

Figure 7.2 Likely P3M3 rating after a successful PRINCE2™ Implementation

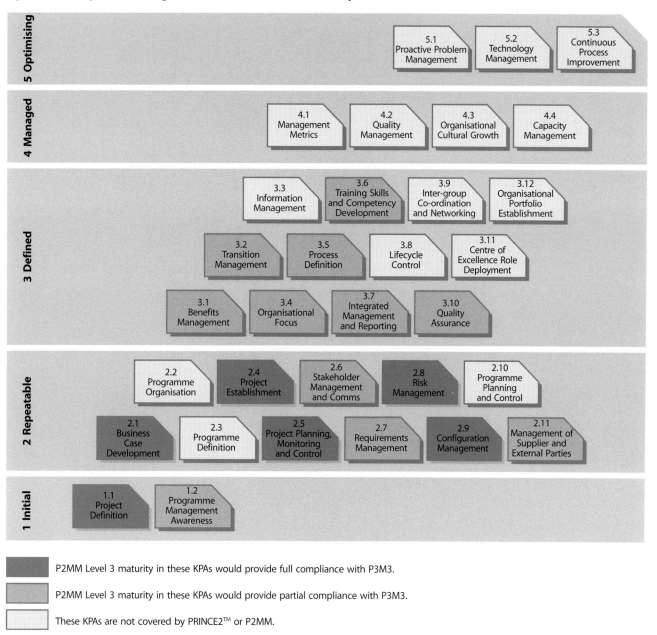

P2MM Level 3 maturity in these KPAs would provide full compliance with P3M3.

P2MM Level 3 maturity in these KPAs would provide partial compliance with P3M3.

These KPAs are not covered by PRINCE2™ or P2MM.

Checklists A

Appendix A: Checklists

A1   PROJECT [MANAGEMENT] DEFINITION (1.1)

Purpose

The purpose of Project Definition is to gain a common and agreed understanding within an organisation that it conducts discrete projects, and that these projects are explicitly recognised. In defining projects the organisation should identify some project objectives. A project should also be managed i.e. subject to at least some management activities, including activity identification. A project is also likely to have some form of project lifecycle, which may be of benefit in high-level planning.

Key Practices	Indicator of conformance
Each project should have agreed objectives and be given the necessary resources to achieve those objectives.	**Project Brief** Is there a statement of scope? Is there an outline plan with resource estimates? Is there a statement of business benefit? Is there a formal approval signature or other evidence of approval (e.g. email, workflow process approval, etc.)?
The organisation should recognise the projects it is undertaking.	**Project Register** Does the organisation have a definition of what should be managed as a project? Does the organisation have a list of projects it is currently engaged on? Does the project list include (as a minimum): project reference, Project Manager, business owner, current status, forecast completion date, expected benefits?
Each Project Manager should be able to identify the key activities that must be carried out.	**Training Records** Is there a list of Project Managers in the organisation and does it include training information? Have the Project Managers had basic training or experience in project management (even if with a previous employer)?

Key Practices	Indicator of conformance
Outline Project Plans are drawn up to distinguish project phases and/or stages.	**Project Plan** Does the project have an outline Project Plan showing project stages? At Level 1, a Gantt chart may be sufficient.
Any changes in project requirements should be recognised.	**All Project Documents** Is there a document history showing revisions to the project's documents?
	Issue Log Are all changes in project requirements recorded somewhere (e.g. in the Issue Log)?
	Do the changes have an associated status to record progress?

A2   DIRECTING A PROJECT (2.1)

Purpose

The purpose of Directing a Project is to ensure that the Project Board exercises overall control over the project and takes responsibility for key decisions.

Key Practices	Indicator of conformance
The Project Board manages by exception.	**PID** Has the Project Board set tolerance levels for the project and are they recorded in the PID?
	Highlight Report Is there a section in the report to warn of potential breaches of tolerance?
	Exception Report If tolerance levels were forecast to be exceeded, was a report sent to the Project Board for review?

Key Practices	Indicator of conformance
The Project Board fulfils its key responsibilities of: ■ Providing overall direction and decision-making ■ Committing appropriate resources to the project.	**PID** Is there representation from the Business, Customer and Supplier on the Project Board? Are the Project Assurance responsibilities of the Project Board clearly defined? **Personal Objectives** Are the project responsibilities for the Project Board members explicitly included in their personal objectives (for major projects)?
The Project Board authorises the Initiation Stage based on the Project Brief, and commits resources to the approved Initiation Stage Plan.	**Project Brief** Is there an outline plan with resource estimates? Is there a formal approval signature or other evidence of approval (e.g. email, workflow process approval, etc.) prior to the initiation stage commencing? **Stage Plan** Is there a plan for the Initiation Stage?
The Project Board authorises the project based on its fit with the business strategies as defined in the PID, and commits resources to the Next Stage Plan.	**Risk Log** Have the major risks been quantified according to their likely impact on the business benefits? **PID** Is there a formal approval signature or other evidence of approval (e.g. email, workflow process approval, etc.)? **Business Case** Does the Business Case include an analysis of the benefits, taking into account the sensitivity to key risks that may affect the project? **Stage Plan** Is there a plan for the next stage?

Key Practices	Indicator of conformance
The Project Board undertakes End Stage Assessments to approve the work to date and provides authority to proceed to the next stage.	**Product Checklist** Were the products identified in the checklist delivered as planned; if not, was approval sought from the Project Board for this variation? **End Stage Report** Has the End Stage Report been produced and does it indicate that the benefits are still on track as defined in the Business Case? **Stage Plan** Is there a plan for the next stage? **Risk Log** Were the risks reviewed at the end of the last stage?
The Project Board monitors progress via Highlight Reports and provides ad hoc direction to the Project Manager.	**Highlight Report** Is the report produced regularly as defined in the PID? Is the report sent to the Project Board? **Ad Hoc Reporting** Are there any records of dialogue with the Project Board members, e.g. emails, notes, key decisions, notification of events, etc.
The Project Board confirms Project Closure based on the End Project Report.	**End Project Report** Is there a plan to support and sustain the technical products delivered by the project? Have all of the technical products been approved and accepted by the customer? Has the Project Board approved the End Project Report and Lessons Learned Report?

A3   INITIATING A PROJECT (2.2)

Purpose

The purpose of Initiating a Project is to ensure that the project is well defined and that there is a sound basis for its management and for the assessment of its overall success.

Key Practices	Indicator of conformance
A Project Brief is produced and approved to provide a full and firm foundation for the initiation of the project.	**Project Brief** Is there a statement of scope? Is there an outline plan with resource estimates? Is there a statement of business benefit?
The initiation stage is formally authorised, based on the Project Brief.	**Project Brief** Is there a formal approval signature or other evidence of approval (e.g. email, workflow process approval, etc.)?
A PID is produced in line with the PRINCE2 standard: ■ The project objectives and benefits are defined and understood ■ The project scope is defined ■ Project tolerance is defined ■ Reporting procedures, contents and frequency are defined ■ Stakeholders' interests are identified and the means of communicating with these stakeholders is defined by the Communications Plan.	**PID** Is the PID based on data from the Risk Log and Business Case? Is there a formal approval signature or other evidence of approval (e.g. email, workflow process approval, etc.)?
Formal approval to proceed to the next stage is provided by the Project Board, based on the PID and the Next Stage Plan: ■ The Project Board accepts accountability for the success of the project and commits the appropriate resources to the project ■ The PID is approved by the Project Board prior to work commencing on specialist products.	**PID** Have tolerances been set for the stage and are they recorded in the Project Plan? Is there a formal approval signature or other evidence of approval (e.g. email, workflow process approval, etc.)? **Stage Plan** Is there a clear statement covering what is to be delivered during the next stage, and has the Stage Plan been approved? Is the Stage Plan consistent with the overall Project Plan?

A4   CONTROLLING A STAGE (2.3)

Purpose
The purpose of Controlling a Stage is to ensure that the Project Manager exercises day-to-day management of the project and reviews progress at the end of each stage.

Key Practices	Indicator of conformance
All work is allocated through the use of Work Packages.	**Work Package** Have the effort, time, cost and quality expectations been defined and are checking methods in place? Is the work achievable within the terms of reference laid down? Have the Work Packages been agreed by both parties? **Team Plans** Is it clear to everyone involved in production what is to be produced, and what has to be done to produce it? **Product Descriptions** Are the Product Descriptions available and clearly understood by all parties involved in product creation and quality checking? **Product Checklist** Does the Product Checklist show to whom the products have been allocated and their status (e.g. pending, in development, in progress, complete)?
Information on actual progress in terms of cost, time and quality is collected, via Checkpoint Reports, and is used to update Stage Plans on a regular basis.	**Stage Plan** Has the Stage or Project Plan been updated since it was approved? **Checkpoint Reports** Are Checkpoint Reports produced in the format and at the frequency defined in the Communications Plan? **Logs** Do the logs show regular updates as expected with a live project?
Project Issues are captured in the Issue Log, examined and resolved on a regular basis.	**Issue Log** Has the Issue Log been updated within the last few weeks?

Key Practices	Indicator of conformance
Progress is reviewed against the Stage Plan on a regular basis to ensure that it is kept within agreed tolerances.	**Checkpoint Reports** Are Checkpoint Reports produced in the format and at the frequency defined in the Communications Plan?
Highlight Reports are produced for the Project Board at agreed intervals and are circulated to other stakeholders as defined by the Communications Plan.	**Highlight Reports** Have Highlight Reports been produced (and sent to key stakeholders) on a regular basis as defined in the Communications Plan? Do the Highlight Reports provide sufficient information for their intended audiences?
Corrective action is taken by the Project Manager where appropriate.	**Risk and Issue Log** Are resolutions to risks and issues recorded? Was an Exception Report issued for those risks or issues that exceeded tolerances?
If it is forecast that a plan will deviate beyond agreed tolerances, an Exception Report is issued to the Project Board.	**Highlight Report** Have any tolerances been exceeded, and if so, was an Exception Report raised and presented to the Project Board? **Exception Report** Does the Exception Report indicate reasons for the project exceeding the tolerances? **Exception Plan** Have any Exception Plans been produced and approved by the Project Board?
At the end of each stage, the Project Manager prepares an End Stage Report in preparation for the End Stage Assessment to sign off completed stages and give approval to proceed.	**End Stage Report** Does the End Stage Report show progress against the baseline Stage Plan? Are any deviations explained? Are forecasts for time, cost and risk to completion included? **Stage Plan** Has the next Stage or Project Plan been produced and submitted for approval?

A5   CLOSING A PROJECT (2.4)

Purpose

The purpose of Closing a Project is to ensure that:

- The project comes to an orderly close
- Unfinished business is formally documented and passed on
- Lessons are learned from the project.

Key Practices	Indicator of conformance
The PID is examined to check the actual results against original expectations.	**End Project Report** Does the End Project Report include a comparison against the plan as agreed in the PID?
Documented confirmation is obtained from the customer that all acceptance criteria have been met.	**Product Checklist** Does the Product Checklist show that all products have been completed?
	Quality Log Does the Quality Log show that all quality and acceptance activities have been completed?
	Acceptance Certificates Are acceptance certificates (or equivalent) in place for the project's products?
An End Project Report is prepared by the Project Manager, evaluating the actual project results versus those envisaged in the PID.	**End Project Report** Has the End Project Report been completed and agreed? Does the End Project Report evaluate whether the benefits stated in the Business Case have been achieved?
The Project Manager prepares Follow-on Action Recommendations based on outstanding Project Issues and risks.	**Follow-on Action Recommendations** Have the Follow-on Action Recommendations been documented, actions identified, agreed and handed over?
	Post-Project Review Plan Is there a Post-Project Review Plan? Do any benefits need to be measured after operational use of the final product?
	Risk Log/Issue Log Are there any risks/issues unresolved in the Risk/Issue Log?

Key Practices	Indicator of conformance
A Lessons Learned Report is prepared based on the Lessons Learned Log maintained during the project.	**Lessons Learned Report** Has the Lessons Learned Report been completed and distributed?
An End Project Notification is prepared to advise the host location that facilities and resources will no longer be required.	**End Project Notification** Have the project resources been informed of the proposed closure?
Management documents are archived.	**Project Documentation** Have all the project documents been archived in accordance with company policy or contract requirements?
	Configuration Management Plan Does the Configuration Management Plan include statements on the archiving requirements and mechanism?

A6   BUSINESS CASE (2.5)

Purpose

The purpose of Business Case is to ensure that there is sufficient justification for undertaking and continuing with the project.

Key Practices	Indicator of conformance
A Business Case is produced which documents the justification for the undertaking of the project based on the estimated cost of the development and implementation against the risks and the anticipated business benefits and savings to be gained.	**Business Case** Is there a project profit and loss statement (or budget statement)? Are the key sensitivities (or risks) analysed to present various benefit profiles?
The Business Case includes the minimum information as defined by PRINCE2; i.e. Reasons, Options, Benefits, Risks, Cost, Timescale, Investment Appraisal and Evaluation.	**Business Case** Does the Business Case include content as defined by PRINCE2?
Costs are based on the Project Plan.	**Project Plan/Business Case** Has the outline budget (from Start-Up) been refined with a detailed budget (from Initiation) as a result of planning?

Key Practices	Indicator of conformance
Benefits are stated in terms that can be measured in the post-project review.	**Business Case** Are each of the benefits stated in the Business Case measurable? Is there a specific person responsible for managing/reporting on the realisation of each benefit?
Investment appraisal is undertaken.	**End Project Report** Does the End Project Report evaluate whether the benefits stated in the Business Case have actually been achieved? Do benefits statements in the project Business Cases drive decision-making within the organisation? Are Business Cases used to measure success?
The Executive of the Project Board accepts ownership of the project's Business Case.	**Business Case** Is the Project Executive accountable for the success of the project?
	Project Register Is there a register of projects showing ownership of the Business Case?

A7   ORGANISATION (2.6)

Purpose

The purpose of Organisation is to establish an appropriate Project Management Team for the project ensuring that resources with the skills and competencies necessary to perform the management activities are made available.

Key Practices	Indicator of conformance
All members of the Project Management Team: ■ Are aware of their roles and responsibilities ■ Understand the processes and procedures used to undertake these responsibilities ■ Are suitably qualified and experienced for their roles.	**PID** Does the PID explicitly state (or refer to) roles and responsibilities for the Project Management Team? **Project Kick-off** Is there evidence of a project kick-off and was it used to brief people involved of their roles and responsibilities and of the processes to be used?

Key Practices	**Indicator of conformance**
A Project Board is appointed to provide overall direction and management of the project: ■ It represents, at managerial level, the business, user and supplier interests ■ The Executive accepts ultimate accountability for the success of the project and commits financial resources ■ The Senior User adequately represents all user areas and commits user resources ■ The role of Senior Supplier is clearly defined and commits supplier resources ■ Project Assurance roles are agreed to ensure adherence to the agreed processes, procedures, tools and standards.	**Organisation Chart** Where do the Project Board members sit within their respective organisations? Are their positions commensurate with the roles they are allocated (e.g. can the Senior User represent the interests of the users)? **Job Descriptions/Objectives** Do Project Board members have the authority to make decisions on behalf of the organisations they represent? Are the project objectives aligned to the personal objectives of each Project Board member?
A single Project Manager is appointed as the focus for day-to-day management of the project: ■ Responsible for the project, producing the required products, to the required standard of quality, within specified constraints of time and cost ■ Responsible for the project delivering an outcome that is capable of achieving the defined benefits.	**Project Register** Is a Project Manager allocated to the project?
The Team Manager role is used where appropriate.	**Stage Plans** Are there any Stage Plans where stages are being used?
Project Support is put in place.	**PID** Is there a published project organisation chart?
Job descriptions are agreed where appropriate, identifying specific responsibilities and the qualifications/experience required. details should be described or referenced in the PID	**PID** Are job descriptions publicly available? Job descriptions may not be appropriate for small projects, but details should be described or referenced in the PID

A8   PLANS/PLANNING (2.7)

Purpose

The purpose of Plans/Planning is to establish credible plans for undertaking the required project and to underpin other project management activities, including the dissemination of planning information to stakeholders and other interested parties.

Key Practices	Indicator of conformance
A Project Plan is created using the PRINCE2 Planning Process and an appropriate form of Product-Based Planning.	**Does the project have the following:** ■ Product Breakdown Structure? ■ Product Flow Diagram? ■ Product Descriptions? ■ Project Plan? ■ Stage Plan (as and when required)? **Project Plan** Are the planning assumptions clearly stated? Are the Stage Plans consistent with the Project Plans?
Strong emphasis is placed on identifying and specifying the products that the project is required to deliver and this provides a firm basis for defining the boundaries/scope of the project.	**Product Description** Does the project have at least one Product Description (for the final product)?
A Product Description is written for each significant product to ensure that it is understood, to describe how the product is to be presented and to define the quality expectations.	**Product Checklist** Is there an entry for all products on the PBS? **Product Description** Is there a Product Description for all items on the Product Checklist?
Where appropriate, Stage Plans, Team Plans and Exception Plans are also produced.	**Does the project have the following:** ■ Stage Plan (as and when required)? ■ Team Plan (as and when required)? ■ Exception Plan?
All plans contain, as a minimum, the following elements: ■ Products, including prerequisites and quality requirements ■ Activities needed to create and validate the quality of the products, plus the dependencies between products and any external dependencies ■ Resources, and time needed for all activities ■ Control points, including tolerances ■ Cost and time schedules.	**Project Plan/Stage Plan** Are the plans produced, reviewed, approved, issued and under change control?

Key Practices	Indicator of conformance
All plans are approved and committed to by the relevant levels of the Project Management Team: ■ For Project Plan and Stages Plans – Project Board and Project Manager ■ For Team Plans – Project Manager and Team Manager.	**Project Plan/Stage Plan** Are Project or Stage Plans produced, reviewed, approved and under change control? Does the distribution list include the relevant recipients?

A9 MANAGEMENT OF RISK (2.8)

Purpose

The purpose of Management of Risk is to identify, analyse, minimise or control the possible adverse effects associated with risks that materialise prior to, or during, the conduct of a project.

Key Practices	Indicator of conformance
The Project Board and Project Manager agree the amount of risk they are prepared to tolerate, i.e. the risk tolerance.	**PID/Stage Plan** Is there a risk tolerance level defined for the project? **Business Case** Does the Business Case include an analysis of benefits, taking into account sensitivity to the effect of key risks that may affect the project?
The responsibilities for the management of risk are agreed between the Project Board and Project Manager.	**Risk Management Plan** Does the project have a Risk Management Plan? Does the project follow a corporate Risk Management Process or does it have its own Risk Management Process? Is there a defined process for dealing with risks that need to be escalated to the Project Board? Is there a project Risk Management Plan in place, allocating the management responsibility for each significant risk? Have the Project Board members been made aware of the risk management planning and those risks that affect them?
An owner is identified for each risk, who should be the person best situated to monitor it.	**Risk Log** Is there an individual assigned to the management and control of each risk in the Risk Log?

Key Practices	Indicator of conformance
Risk analysis is undertaken, as a minimum during initiation and at the end of every stage, consisting of: ■ Identifying risks ■ Evaluating risks, taking into account impact, probability and proximity ■ Identifying suitable responses, i.e. prevention, reduction, transference, acceptance or contingency ■ Selecting responses.	**Risk Log** Are major project risks identified and mitigation actions put in place? Have the impact, probability and proximity of all risks in the Risk Log been evaluated? Is there evidence that the Risk Log was reviewed and updated at the end of the last stage? Were any new risks added to the Risk Log at the last review? Does the Risk Log contain appropriate analysis as described in the Risk Management Plan (or in the corporate Risk Management Process)? Were the risks reassessed when the plans last changed?
Risk management is undertaken on an ongoing basis, consisting of: ■ Planning and resourcing selected responses ■ Monitoring and reporting ■ A Risk Log is maintained to hold information about risk, risk analysis, countermeasures and status.	**Risk Log** Is there evidence that the Risk Log was reviewed on a regular basis (period should be defined in the Risk Plan, but should be at least monthly)? Were the major risks escalated to the Project Board for consideration? Have contingency plans been put in place for any risks now regarded as serious? **PID** Are any contingencies described for the project's major risks?

A10 CONTROLS (2.9)

Purpose

The purpose of Controls is to provide adequate visibility into actual project progress so that management can take effective action if the project's performance deviates significantly from the Project Plans.

Key Practices	Indicator of conformance
The Project Board exercises control by way of: ■ Project Initiation (during which the Project Plan is produced and the use of Stages and Tolerances are agreed with the Project Manager) ■ End Stage Assessments ■ Highlight Reports ■ Exception Reports ■ Exception Assessments.	**Daily Log** Are all approvals recorded? **Are there minutes/records of ...** Initiation Review, End Stage Assessments, End Project Review? **Highlight Reports** Have Highlight Reports been produced at the frequency specified in the PID? **Exception Report** Did the Project Board respond to the Exception Report and provide guidance and direction for its resolution?
The Project Manager exercises control by the appropriate use of PRINCE2 management products, for example: ■ Stage Plans ■ Product Descriptions ■ Work Packages ■ Checkpoint Reports ■ Quality Log ■ Daily Log ■ Issue and Risk Logs.	**Project File** Does the Project File contain up-to-date: ■ Stage Plans? ■ Product Descriptions? ■ Work Packages? ■ Checkpoint Reports? ■ Quality Log? ■ Daily Log? ■ Issue and Risk Logs?

A11 QUALITY MANAGEMENT (2.10)

Purpose

The purpose of Quality Management is to provide management with the confidence that the project processes are resulting in products of a suitable level of quality.

Key Practices	Indicator of conformance
Customer's quality expectations and acceptance criteria are defined and agreed with the Senior User and are captured in the Project Quality Plan.	**Project Quality Plan** Has the customer specified any quality expectations? Is there a reference to the customer's Quality Management System? **Product Descriptions** Have Quality Criteria been defined for each Product? **Quality Log** Is the Quality Log up to date? Are quality assurance (external to the project) role holders satisfied with their involvement?
A Project Quality Plan is produced which defines, in general terms, how the project will meet the customer's quality expectations.	**Project Quality Plan** Is there a Project Quality Plan? Does the Project Quality Plan specify the quality checking methods to be used? Are corporate Quality Management Systems referenced? Are named individuals assigned quality roles?
Each Stage Plan specifies in detail the required quality activities and resources, with the detailed quality criteria shown in the Product Descriptions.	**Stage Plan** Does the current Stage Plan indicate quality requirements, and is sufficient time specifically devoted to quality checking?

Key Practices	Indicator of conformance
The quality of products is verified against quality criteria as part of Executing Work Packages, and the results of these quality controls are recorded in the Quality Log.	**Quality Log** Is the Quality Log being used to record results of quality controls? Have the follow-on actions been progressed and signed off as completed? **Work Package** Do Work Packages indicate the quality requirements?
All necessary stakeholders are involved in quality control activities.	**Communications Plan/Project Quality Plan** Are the stakeholders defined in the Communications Plan also included in the Project Quality Plan?
Identified problems with quality are raised as Project Issues, captured, examined and, if necessary, escalated to the Project Board.	**Issue Log** Are there any issues relating to quality in the Issue Log?

A12 CONFIGURATION MANAGEMENT AND CHANGE CONTROL (2.11)

Purpose

The purpose of Configuration Management and Change Control is to establish and maintain the integrity of the project documentation and specialist products throughout the life of the project, and to ensure that decisions on the implementation of changes are based on a sound assessment of the implications of such changes.

Key Practices	Indicator of conformance
A Configuration Management Plan is produced which identifies how and by whom the project's products will be controlled and protected. This should identify the person with responsibility for undertaking the role of Configuration Librarian.	**PID** Does the PID contain or refer to the Configuration Management Plan? Does the PID show how configuration management will be applied to management products as well as specialist products? **Project File** Is there a document describing project filing, and who is responsible for maintaining it? Are old versions clearly identified and accessible in the file?

Key Practices	Indicator of conformance
All products are uniquely identified and the relationships between products established.	**Product Checklist** Are all products uniquely identified?
All products are baselined following the successful completion of quality control: ■ Products are submitted to the Configuration Librarian ■ Where practical, master copies are retained and copies alone are issued.	**Product Checklist** Is the status shown for all products?
Product records are kept up-to-date to enable accurate status accounting.	**Product Checklist** Is the status shown for all products?
Configuration Audits are undertaken at the end of every stage.	**Quality Log** Is there any evidence of a Configuration Audit?
All changes are dealt with as types of Project Issue and a record is maintained through the Issue Log.	**Issue Log** Does the Issue Log show the type of issue and its status? **PID** Does the PID describe the issue and change process?
The authority for approving or rejecting Project Issues is decided on by the Project Board during the initiation stage.	**PID** Does the PID describe the issue and change process and has it been approved by the Project Board?
Members of the Project Board are involved in making decisions on Requests for Change where the Project Board members may be affected.	**PID** Does the PID describe the issue and change process including the categorisation of issues that need Project Board decisions?

A13 ORGANISATIONAL FOCUS (3.1)

Purpose

The purpose of Organisational Focus is to establish the organisational responsibility for the adoption of PRINCE2 with the aim of improving the organisation's overall project management capability.

Key Practices	Indicator of conformance
There is a defined role within the organisation with responsibility for coordinating the use of PRINCE2.	**Organisation Chart** Does the chart show a methodology owner?
This role has the appropriate level of authority to mandate the use of PRINCE2 on all projects within the organisation.	**PID** Is the person to whom the Project Executive reports, part of corporate ownership (board of directors)? **Follow-on Action Recommendations** Is there a recommendation stating how local sponsors/champions ensure that PRINCE2 is used during business-as-usual? Post-Project Review Plan Is there a statement about how project benefits will be assessed post-project closure and who is responsible for them?
Sufficient time/resource is made available to make this role effective and to provide support/mentoring to Project Managers and project teams.	**Organisation Chart** Does the chart show a team of people who can provide support to all parts of the organisation? Is the team focussed on developing the method and providing mentoring?
Project Managers consistently apply the PRINCE2 method to help them produce the required project deliverables.	**Product Description** Is there a Product Description for each product in the project? **Product Checklist** Does the checklist identify project deliverables? **Quality Log** Was there any formal review of the deliverables? **PID** Is someone appointed to perform Project Assurance?

Key Practices	Indicator of conformance
Data is collected to enable improvements to the use of PRINCE2 to be made.	**Lessons Learned** Are Lessons Learned produced for each project? Are they collated and reviewed? **Issue Log** Is there a place where users' feedback on the methodology can be recorded?
The effectiveness of PRINCE2 is reviewed at least annually, with input from Project Board members.	**Annual Review: Agenda/Minutes/Actions** Agenda: does the invitation/attendee list include members of the Project Boards? Minutes: are there still more benefits to be accrued? Actions: is there an action plan?
Recommendations from these reviews are incorporated into an improvement plan that is implemented and reviewed on an ongoing basis.	**Annual Review: Agenda/Minutes/Actions** Are there any actions resulting from Issue Log entries? Are there any actions resulting from Issue Log entries? Is there an Improvement Roadmap/Plan? Are Improvement Plans referenced in the Business Unit Development Plan?

A14 TAILORING OF PRINCE2 (3.2)

Purpose

The purpose of Tailoring of PRINCE2 is to align the project management method to the other business processes that govern and support the project, and to develop and maintain a set of project management process assets that can be used by all projects within the organisation to improve project performance.

Key Practices	Indicator of conformance
PRINCE2 is tailored to meet the specific needs of the organisation in terms of its policies, business goals, strategies and priorities.	**Project Management Handbook** Are some of the templates mandatory for use on all projects? Are some of the PRINCE2 processes embedded within core business systems processes?
Senior management within the organisation approves the tailoring of the PRINCE2 method.	**Project Management Handbook** Is there an approved Project Management Handbook based on PRINCE2? Has the Project Management Handbook been regularly reviewed and updated?
This tailoring is documented and includes the following: ■ Description of project roles ■ Planning standards ■ Guidance on the use of project management tools ■ A library of standard Management Product Descriptions, derived from the PRINCE2 Product Outlines in Appendix A of the PRINCE2 manual.	**Project Management Handbook** Does the handbook cover the prescribed areas? Are some of the templates mandatory for all projects?
Senior management, in a Project Board role, adopts PRINCE2 and ensures that the Project Manager follows the method.	**Confirmed by observation**
Lessons Learned on individual projects are used to identify areas where further tailoring would improve the use of PRINCE2.	**Improvement Plan** Is there an Improvement Plan based on a review of Lessons Learned? **Lessons Learned** Is there a searchable repository of Lessons Learned from all projects in the organisation?
Project Boards may adapt the use of PRINCE2 to meet individual project needs, based on documented guidance.	Is there any notion of project scaling within the organisation – i.e. do the key attributes of a project drive the amount of process required for implementation?

A15 TRAINING IN PRINCE2 (3.3)

Purpose

The purpose of Training in PRINCE2 is to develop the skills and knowledge of all members of the Project Management Team so that they can perform their roles effectively and efficiently.

Key Practices	Indicator of conformance
Training needs are identified and documented for each of the Project Management Team roles: ■ Project Board members (including any project assurance roles) are trained to understand their roles and responsibilities and to perform the Directing a Project process ■ Project Managers are trained to Practitioner Level ■ Team Managers and Project Support staff are trained to Foundation Level.	**Training Plan** Are there a number of different training events available: awareness, formal PRINCE2 accreditation to Foundation and Practitioner Level? Is there specialist training for the Project Board and people who carry out quality assurance? Does the plan indicate the number of events required, timing and location, etc.? **Training Records** Is training information captured on each appropriate person to determine training requirements?
Appropriate training in the use of PRINCE2 is provided to everyone undertaking a Project Management Team role, and this is provided in a timely fashion.	**Personal Development Plan** Does the Project Management Team have appropriate PRINCE2 training included in their personal development plan?
Where appropriate, skills and competencies are assessed at the end of each PRINCE2 training event.	**Assessments** Was any post-course assessments performed?
The training covers general principles of PRINCE2 and how the method has been tailored for use within the organisation.	**Training Plan** Is there an overview event for all project management staff in the organisation to attend?
The overall effectiveness of the PRINCE2 training is measured on an ongoing basis.	**Training Feedback Form** Has each candidate filled in a feedback form at the end of training?
Does the form have measurement scoring criteria to record candidates' feedback as a well as free-text areas? training event?	**Training Report** Is a consolidated training report produced at the end of each training event?

A16 INTEGRATED MANAGEMENT (3.4)

Purpose
The purpose of Integrated Management is to ensure that all project activities form a coherent set based on the PRINCE2 method. It necessitates the development of a Project Initiation Document that takes into account the project's size, schedule and staffing. The emphasis is on anticipating problems and minimising their effects.

Key Practices	Indicator of conformance
There is an organisational policy requiring all projects to use PRINCE2. In particular: ■ Every project has an Initiation Stage ■ During this stage a PID is produced that identifies the customer's quality expectations and acceptance criteria ■ Tolerances are agreed by all members of the Project Management Team ■ Projects are broken down into subsequent stages that are planned, monitored and controlled in accordance with PRINCE2 ■ Formal reviews are undertaken at the end of each stage ■ Projects are closed in an orderly fashion as prescribed by PRINCE2.	**Projects Policy Statement** Is there a published and agreed directive stating that the organisation is to use PRINCE2 and establishing the minimum criteria for conformance?
Any variations from PRINCE2 are documented and approved.	**Project Management Handbook** Is there a published handbook advising users on how to apply PRINCE2 (or local variations)? Has the handbook been regularly reviewed and updated?
Adequate resources are provided to enable projects to be managed in accordance with PRINCE2.	**Resource Allocation** Does the organisation have a record of which members of staff are working on which projects?

A17 QUALITY ASSURANCE (3.5)

Purpose

The purpose of Quality Assurance is to provide an organisational assurance that the project has suitable quality plans and measures, in line with the tailored PRINCE2 method, to ensure that the project processes are suitably controlled and are likely to result in products that meet explicit quality criteria as defined by Product Descriptions.

Key Practices	Indicator of conformance
The Quality Assurance Group monitors the application of PRINCE2 across all projects within the organisation.	**Quality Assurance Plan** Does the organisation define how it will assure the application of PRINCE2? Does the company have a schedule of project audits (or equivalent)? **Project Register** Has the Project Register been extended to include the presence of key documents as defined by the project type (e.g. a PID)?
The Quality Assurance Group is independent of the organisation's project and operational activities.	**Quality Assurance Plan** Is the group set up to monitor Quality Assurance independent of the team that developed or operates the processes?
The Quality Assurance Group reviews Project Quality Plans and makes recommendations to improve the plans and, consequently, the likelihood of quality deliverables.	**Project Quality Plans (sample of)** Does the document history or approvals section show a review of the Project Quality Plans by the Quality Assurance function? **Quality Assurance Report** Does the Quality Assurance Report detail the number of projects with Project Quality Plans and their conformance? Have the recommendations from the Quality Assurance Report been followed up?

Key Practices	Indicator of conformance
Quality Assurance reviews assess whether: ■ The appropriate skills and competencies are in place ■ Risks are being managed effectively ■ Feasible and economic contingency measures are in place.	Quality Assurance Report Have there been formal reviews of projects within the organisation conducted by the Quality Assurance Group or an independent body? Is there a published report stating the findings and recommendations of the review group?
Peer reviews are conducted to encourage shared learning across projects. Peer reviews: ■ Are led by trained review leaders ■ Focus on the project deliverables ■ Are adequately resourced.	**Quality Logs (sample of)** Do Quality Logs include records of peer reviews (either planned or actual)? **Quality Assurance Report** Have there been peer reviews of projects within the organisation?

More on maturity models and P2MM

B

Appendix B: More on maturity models and P2MM

The Software Engineering Institute (SEI) developed the first Capability Maturity Model® (CMM®) in the 1980s based on earlier work by quality guru Phil Crosby. This was a result of research indicating that the quality of software applications directly related to the quality of the processes used to develop them.

Therefore by inspecting the quality of an organisation's development processes it is possible to predict the likely quality of the applications it develops. CMM® was originally intended as a tool for the US Government to evaluate the ability of contractors to deliver a software project. Although they originated in the software development industry, maturity models are now widely used as a general model of the maturity of processes (e.g. within project and programme management).

Figure B.1 shows how the use of levels enables management to assess overall maturity and prioritise improvement initiatives. Breaking down maturity levels into Key Process Areas (KPA) that contain Key Practices provides focus for planning and an objective method of assessment against best practice.

Each KPA contains Key Practices that contribute to process capability. These Key Practices are organised by common features, which will help an organisation when attempting to implement and embed them.

Additionally, each KPA is defined by its goal, i.e. the purpose of the process area, and details what the organisation should expect to achieve by gaining maturity in that KPA.

Improvement in multiple KPAs needs to take place to progress to the next level of maturity. KPAs within a level are defined by the characterisation of that level. For example, within P2MM, Quality Management is a Level 2 KPA, which means it is defined with the characteristics of a process that can be *repeatedly* applied (even if inconsistently so), whereas Quality Assurance is a Level 3 KPA with the characteristics of a defined process that is *consistently* applied across all projects.

P2MM differs from other maturity models in that it contains only high-level descriptions of the Key Practices to avoid duplication of the PRINCE2 manual (which already codifies a large number of the best practices). P2MM is a much simplified maturity model, therefore, and only contains three levels of maturity. P2MM is not organised by common features as much of the detail is contained in the PRINCE2 manual. Instead, each KPA contains a purpose and a set of Key Practices (see Figure B.2).

P2MM is derived from the PRINCE2 manual3, and the Portfolio, Programme and Project Management Maturity Model (P3M3)[2], which itself is derived from SEI's Capability Maturity Model® Integration (CMMI®)[10].

The OGC's accreditation partner the APM Group has developed an assessment method11 that correlates observed behaviour with the Key Practices, and therefore with KPAs, and in turn with the maturity level of an organisation. The first set of assessments was used to calibrate the question set and provide feedback on the model itself. This feedback loop and updates to the PRINCE2 manual will ensure that P2MM continues to evolve to represent current best practices based on the collective experiences and knowledge of the PRINCE2 community (see Figure B.3).

Figure B.1 Maturity model structure

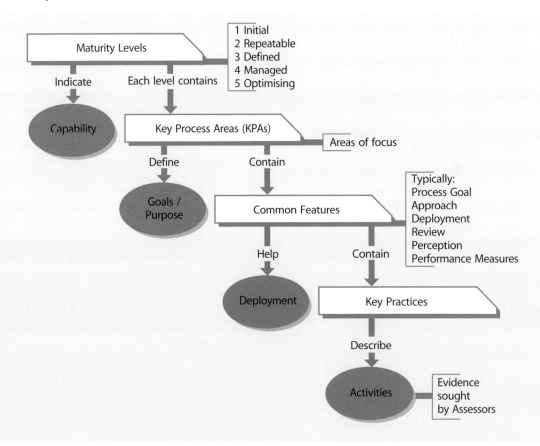

Figure B.2 How P2MM is applied to the CMMI® structure

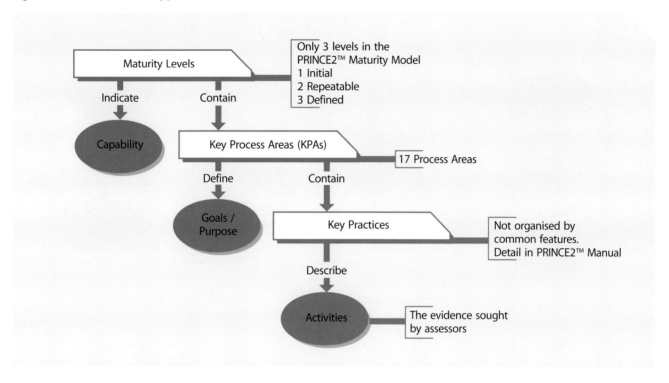

Figure B.3 P2MM derivation and continuous evolution

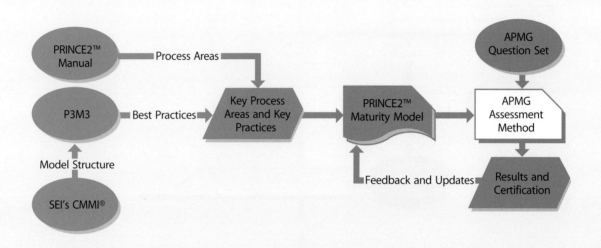

About the authors

Appendix C: About the authors

ANDY MURRAY

Andy Murray is a Chartered Director and PRINCE2 Registered Consultant (P2RC), and has worked in the field of projects and programmes for over 15 years.

He is currently a director of Outperform UK Ltd (www.outperform.co.uk), an Accredited Consulting Organisation (ACO) licensed to consult in the OGC's best practice trilogy of PRINCE2, MSP and M_o_R.

Andy was an early adopter of PRINCE2 back in 1997, and has been helping organisations implement and gain value from PRINCE2 ever since. He has helped implement PRINCE2 in numerous organisations in more than a dozen countries. Andy has been using maturity models as a consulting aid for more than five years, as a tool to help diagnose an organisation's strengths and weaknesses, prioritise improvement initiatives and measure progress. Andy has used the OGC's PRINCE2 Maturity Model (P2MM) and Portfolio, Programme and Project Management Maturity Model (P3M3) as a means to benchmark organisations via the APM Group assessment process and to define improvement plans.

Andy is the Lead Author for the PRINCE2 Refresh Project, which started in May 2007.

MIKE WARD

Mike Ward is a Business Change Manager with knowledge and experience of a wide variety of best practice methods for the management of projects and programmes. His experience as a CMM® assessor and Six Sigma practitioner is being used to help clients undergo business change.

He is currently a director of Outperform UK Ltd (www.outperform.co.uk), an Accredited Consulting Organisation (ACO) licensed to consult in the OGC's best practice trilogy of PRINCE2, MSP and M_o_R.

Mike has worked in the IT industry for over 25 years, holding positions in programme management, project management and R&D, specializing in the areas of professional services, project management methods and computer architectures. He has considerable experience in managing enterprise-scale international collaborative programmes in Europe and the US.

Mike is a Project and Programme Management Registered Consultant (PPMRC) and a PRINCE2 Registered Consultant (P2RC).

Further information

Further information

The publications and links identified in this section will help you achieve a greater level of understanding of PRINCE2 and how to apply it effectively and will also put you in contact with the rest of the PRINCE2 community. Details of the reports referenced throughout this text are provided in the References section. There are also links to websites where you can find out more about maturity models in general.

REFERENCES

1   PRINCE2™ Maturity Model, March 2006, Version 1.0.

2   Portfolio, Programme and Project Management Maturity Model, February 2006, Version 1.0.

3   *Managing Successful Projects Using PRINCE2™*, 2005 edition, ISBN 9780113309467.

4   *Directing Change – A Guide to Governance of Project Management* (reprinted with minor revisions 2005), APM Governance SIG, ISBN 9781903494158.

5   *Delivering Successful IT-Enabled Business Change*, National Audit Office, report by the Comptroller and Auditor General HC 33-I Session 2006-2007, 17 November 2006. Printed in the UK for the TSO (The Stationery Office Ltd.) on behalf of the Controller of Her Majesty's Stationery Office, 5461135 11/06 65536.

6   *Management of Risk: Guidance for Practitioners*, 2007, ISBN 9780113310388.

7   Vodafone case study (ILX Customer Projects), 2005.

8   Pension Protection Fund case study (Kate Winter), 2006.

9   Port of Rotterdam case study (Expecto), 2005.

10 CMMI-DEV v1.2, August 2006.

11 The APM Group Ltd's Assessment Model for Portfolio, Programme and Project Management, its PRINCE2™ Maturity Model and their Benefits to Organisations, Alan Harpham, Chairman of the APM Group Ltd.

PUBLICATIONS

If you haven't already got a copy of this, it's a 'must have' – the PRINCE2 manual:

Managing Successful Projects with PRINCE2™, ISBN 9780113309467

Tailoring PRINCE2™, ISBN 9780113308972

Business Benefits through Programme and Project Management, ISBN 9780113310258

People Issues and PRINCE2™, ISBN 9780113308965

PRINCE2™ for the Project Executive: practical advice for achieving project governance, ISBN 9780113309672

Publications are available in a variety of formats and can be purchased from www.best-management-practice.com

Other OGC guidance of interest:

Managing Successful Programmes (MSP), ISBN 9780113309177

Management of Risk: Guidance for Practitioners (M_o_R®), ISBN 9780113310388

WEB LINKS

The Best Management Practice website – the OGC official umbrella site dedicated to making access to the guidance quick and easy – provides support for all levels of adoption of the OGC Best Practice guidance.

www.best-management-practice.com

Official User Group:
www.usergroup.org.uk

The P3M3/P2MM models:
www.ogc.gov.uk

The P3M3/P2MM accreditation details:
www.apmgroup.co.uk

The Standard CMM Assessment Method for Process Improvement (SCAMPI):
www.sei.cmu.edu

SEI's data on performance improvement:
www.sei.cmu.edu/cmmi/results

Directing Change – A Guide to Governance of Project Management:
www.apm.org.uk

Glossary

Acronyms list

ACO	Accredited Consulting Organisation
APM	Association for Project Management
APM Group	APM Group Ltd, the OGC's accreditation partner
CMM®, CMMI®	Capability Maturity Model® and Capability Maturity Model® Integration – developed by the Software Engineering Institute (SEI)
CoE	Centre of excellence
CP	'Closing a Project' – a set of processes in the PRINCE2 method.
CQE	Customer's quality expectations
DP1	The first process involved in 'Directing a Project' called 'Authorising Initiation'
DP2	The second process involved in 'Directing a Project' called 'Authorising a Project'
DP3	The third process involved in 'Directing a Project' called 'Authorising a Stage or Exception Plan'
ICT	Information and communication technology
IP	'Initiating a Project' – a set of processes in the PRINCE2 method.
KPA	Key Process Area
NAO	National Audit Office
OGC	Office of Government Commerce
P1M3	Project Management Maturity Model

P2, PRINCE2™	The standard UK government method for project management that provides a process-based framework for setting up and controlling projects; the acronym stands for 'projects in controlled environments'
P2M3	Programme and Project Management Maturity Model
P2MM	PRINCE2 Maturity Model
P2RC	PRINCE2 Registered Consultant
P3M3	Portfolio, Programme and Project Management Maturity Model
PBS	Product Breakdown Structure
PD	Product Description
PFD	Product Flow Diagram
PID	Project Initiation Document
PINO	PRINCE in Name Only
PMO	Project management office
PPF	Pension Protection Fund
PPMRC	Project and Programme Management Registered Consultant
PPSO	Programme and project support office
PSO	Project support office
QMS	Quality Management System
RFC	Request for Change
ROI	Return on investment
SEI	Software Engineering Institute

SRO	Senior Responsible Owner
SS	Senior Supplier
SU	Senior User
SU1	The first process involved in 'Starting up a Project' called 'Appointing an Executive and a Project Manager'
SU2	The second process involved in 'Starting up a Project' called 'Designing a Project Management Team'
SU3	The third process involved in 'Starting up a Project' called 'Appointing a Project Management Team'
UKAS	United Kingdom Accreditation Service

Definitions list

Acceptance criteria
A prioritised list of criteria that the final product(s) must meet before the customer will accept them.

Accredited Consulting Organisation
An organisation assessed by the APM Group Ltd and recommended by OGC that provides consulting services in one or more of the OGC's best practice products (e.g. PRINCE2) delivered by Registered Consultants.

Authority matrix
A table describing a list of delegated authority for approvals; may be referred to as a Scheme of Delegated Authority (SODA).

Business Case
The justification for an initiative (programme, project, activity), which typically contains costs, benefits, risks and timescales and against which continuing viability is tested.

Checkpoint Report
A progress report of the information gathered at a checkpoint meeting, which is given by a team to the Project Manager and provides reporting data as defined in the Work Package.

Capability Maturity Model
Capability Maturity Model Integration
Developed by the Software Engineering Institute (SEI).

Combined Code
The 'Combined Code on Corporate Governance' sets out standards of good practice in relation to issues such as board composition and development, remuneration, accountability and audit and relations with shareholders.

Configuration Item
An item that is under change control and therefore recorded in the Product Checklist.

Configuration Item Record
A record of the information required about a product's status (links to Product Descriptions, Requests for Change, Issues, Owners, version numbers, etc.).

Customer's quality expectations
A statement from the customer about the quality expected from the final product.

Daily Log
A record of jobs to do or to check that others have done, commitments from the author or others, important events, decisions or discussions.

Deliverables
Items that the project has to create as part of the requirements. It may be part of the final outcome or an intermediate element on which one or more subsequent deliverables depend. According to the type of project, another name for a deliverable is product.

Enterprise Planning Tool
A project and portfolio management solution covering time/resource/cost management along with additional functions such as scope management, procurement management, communications management, risk management, quality management and integration management.

Exception Plan
This is a plan that often follows an Exception Report. For a Team Plan exception, it covers the period from the present to the end of the Work Package; for a Stage Plan exception, it covers the period from the

present to the end of the current stage. If the exception were at a project level, the Project Plan would be replaced.

Exception Report

Description of the exception situation, its impact, options, the recommendation and impact of the recommendation to the Project Board.

Executive

The individual with overall responsibility for ensuring that a project meets its objectives and delivers the projected benefits. This individual should ensure that the project or programme maintains its business focus, that it has clear authority and that the work, including risks, is actively managed. The Executive is the chairperson of the Project Board, representing the customer, and is the owner of the Business Case. *See also* Project Executive.

Fishbone diagram

An Ishikawa diagram, also known as a fishbone diagram or cause and effect diagram, is a diagram that shows the causes of a certain event.

Gateway Review

The OGC Gateway Review Process examines a programme or project at critical stages in its lifecycle, to provide assurance that it can progress successfully to the next stage.

Highlight Report

A time-driven report from the Project Manager to the Project Board on stage progress.

Ishikawa diagram

An Ishikawa diagram, also known as a fishbone diagram or cause and effect diagram, is a diagram that shows the causes of a certain event.

Issue Log

Contains all Project Issues, including Requests for Change raised during the project.

Key Practices

The Key Practices describe the infrastructure and activities that contribute most to the effective implementation and institutionalisation of the Key Process Area.

Key Process Area

A KPA is a cluster of best practices in an area, which when implemented collectively satisfy a set of goals considered important for making significant improvement in that area.

Lessons Learned Log

An informal collection of good and bad lessons learned about the management and specialist processes and products as the project progresses.

Management product

Products produced and delivered by the Project Manager as defined in PRINCE2.

Off-specification

Something that should be provided by the project, but currently is not (or is forecast not to be) provided.

Outcome

The result of change, normally affecting real-world behaviour and/or circumstances. Outcomes are desired when a change is conceived. Outcomes are achieved as a result of the activities undertaken to effect the change.

Output

See Products.

Product Breakdown Structure

A hierarchy of all the products to be produced during a plan.

Product Checklist

A list of the major products of a plan, plus key dates in their delivery.

Product Description

A description of a product's purpose, composition, derivation and quality criteria. It is produced at planning time, as soon as possible after the need for the product is identified.

Product Flow Diagram

A diagram showing the sequence of production and interdependencies of the products listed in a Product Breakdown Structure.

Products

An input or output, whether tangible or intangible, that can be described in advance, created and tested. Also known as an output or deliverable.

Project Brief

A statement that describes the purpose, cost, time and performance requirements/constraints for a project.

Project Executive

Also known as the Executive. The single individual with overall responsibility for ensuring that a project meets its objectives and delivers the projected benefits.

Project Initiation Document

A logical document that brings together the key information needed to start the project on a sound basis and to convey that information to all concerned with the project.

Project Issue

A term used to cover any concern, query, Request for Change, suggestion or off-specification raised during the project.

Project Plan

A high-level plan showing the major products of the project, when they will be delivered and at what cost.

Project Quality Plan

A plan defining the key quality criteria, quality control and audit processes to be applied to project management and specialist work in the PRINCE2 project.

Quality Log

Contains all planned and completed quality activities.

Quality Management System

The complete set of quality standards, procedures and responsibilities for a site or organisation.

Request for Change

A means of proposing a modification to the current specification of a product. It is one type of Project Issue.

Return on investment

In finance, the rate of return (ROR), return on investment (ROI), or return, is a comparison of the money earned (or lost) on an investment with the amount of money invested. Real-world considerations include further adjustments for income taxes and transaction costs.

Risk

An uncertain event or set of events that, should it occur, will have an effect on the achievement of objectives. A risk is measured by a combination of the probability of a perceived threat or opportunity occurring and the magnitude of its impact on objectives.

Risk Log

A record of all identified risks relating to an initiative with their status and history. Also called a Risk Register.

Senior Responsible Owner

The single individual with overall responsibility for ensuring that a project or programme meets its objectives and delivers the projected benefits.

Senior Supplier

The Project Board role that provides knowledge and experience of the main discipline(s) involved in the production of the project's deliverable(s). Represents the supplier interests within the project and provides supplier resources.

Senior User

The Project Board role accountable for ensuring that user needs are specified correctly and that the solution meets those needs.

Software Engineering Institute

The SEI is a US federally funded research and development centre conducting software engineering research in acquisition, architecture and product lines, process improvement and performance measurement, security, and system interoperability and dependability. They are the originators of the Capability Maturity Model".

Specialist product

Products produced and delivered by the technical manager as defined by the specialist product lifecycle.

Stage Plan

A detailed plan describing the products that will be produced, when, by whom, and within which tolerances.

Tolerance

The permissible deviation above and below a plan's estimate of time and cost without escalating the deviation to the next level of management.

United Kingdom Accreditation Service

The organisation that certifies accreditation bodies.

Work Package

The set of information relevant to the creation of one or more products.

Index

Index